YUKON WATER STUDIES

Aluminum Smelting in the Yukon: An Assessment of Economic Viability

by
John P. Thompson

Westwater Research Centre
The University of British Columbia
Vancouver, B.C. V6T 1W5

Westwater Research Centre was established in 1971. Its function is to conduct interdisciplinary research on the management of water and associated resources. The Centre aims to provide an improved foundation for decisions about policies and institutional arrangements through rigorous analysis of the alternative courses of action that might be undertaken. Results of research are published in books, a periodical bulletin, *Westwater,* and a series of reports; publications presently available are listed at the back of this book.

Canadian Arctic Resources Committee
46 Elgin Street, Room 11
Ottawa, Ontario   K1P 5K6

The Canadian Arctic Resources Committee has helped to fund and publish this volume in the Yukon Water Study Series in the belief that this research deserves immediate consideration by those concerned with the future of the Yukon Water Resources.

The committee regards this volume as a "working" publication, with the content remaining the sole responsibility of the author.

CARC's 1977-1982 Publishing Programme is made possible by a grant from the Richard and Jean Ivey Fund

Front Cover Design: Itsuo Yesaki
Printing: BEST-Printer Co. Ltd.

Aluminum Smelting in the Yukon:
An Assessment of Economic Viability

Thompson, J.P. (John Payson), 1952-
    Aluminum Smelting in the Yukon

        (Information report/Westwater Research
    Centre, ISSN 0711-1215; no. 1)
        ISBN 0-920146-06-6

        1. Aluminum industry and trade - Yukon
    Territory. 2. Aluminum plants - Yukon
    Territory. I. Westwater Research Centre.
    II. Title. III. Series: Information report
    (Westwater Research Centre); no. 1
    HD9539.A63C397   338.2'74926'097191
                                    C81-091379-8

The purpose of the book is to examine the conditions under which an aluminum smelter might be viable in the Yukon Territory. This viability is assessed in two ways. First, a description of the world aluminum industry is provided to determine whether or not a Yukon smelter would be able to operate within present and future aluminum supply/demand balances. Secondly, a hypothetical smelter is described in terms of actual capital and operating costs and revenues to determine the range of electric power costs in which such a smelter would be economically feasible. Future development of a smelter in the Yukon will then largely depend on how the predicted cost of electric power demanded by the smelter relates to the eventual cost of power to be supplied from any of the Yukon hydrolectric projects now under consideration by the Northern Canada Power Commission.

FOREWORD

Electric power demand in the Yukon is relatively modest at the present time. For example in 1978 the peak demand was only 63.5 MW (megawatts) and is only expected to increase to less than 100 MW by 1983. Unless a major new use for electric power in the Yukon arises the outlook is that peak capacity requirements will total only about 131 MW by 1998 (Foster Research, Forecast Electric Energy Requirements in the Yukon Territory, 1979-1998).

The amount of electric power use in a region is a major determinant of cost because the unit cost of electric power, generally speaking, declines rapidly with the increased size of generating facilities. The modest size of existing facilities is one major reason that electric power prices are relatively high in the Yukon in comparison with prices in southern Canada. If larger scale facilities could be justified, it is only logical to conclude that power could be priced at a lower level. This would benefit existing consumers and would make those economic activities for which electric power costs are an important element of production costs more competitive with industry in southern Canada.

The foregoing considerations together with the employment that a large scale power user would generate has prompted those interested in stimulating economic growth in the Yukon to be on the look-out for a large power user. An aluminum smelter is a potential candidate for such a role. As this report indicates, a smelter large enough to take advantage of economies of scale and current technologies would require about 320 MW of power. It would employ a work force of about 1200 people and the goods and services this work force would require would probably result in an equal increase in employment in the service industries. Furthermore the demand for aluminum throughout the world is rising because, among other reasons, the use of light metals in automobile production is increasing..

Figure III-1 on page 84 provides a variety of estimates of the maximum electricity rates that a Yukon aluminum smelter could afford, given several alternative assumptions about annual increases in aluminum prices and the capacity factor at which the plant would operate. These estimates range between 14 mills and 70 mills at 1980 price levels depending upon the assumptions made. In terms of electric energy supply costs, a report by Montreal Engineering Company on the Mid-Yukon Project estimated that the cost of firm energy from a plant with a capacity of 480 MW (and assuming an interest rate on capital of 12%) would be 31 mills at 1980 price levels.

The importance of potential large power users to water resources planning in the Yukon led Westwater to commission the study that resulted in this report, which aims to illuminate the economic viability of establishing and operating an aluminum smelter in the Yukon. It is not a detailed feasibility study, but is based largely on available literature describing the aluminum industry, data drawn from various sources on production, use and markets for aluminum, and consultation with industry representatives. Thus, the estimates derived from the analyses must be viewed as good approximations rather than hard estimates on which specific investment decisions can be based. It is believed, however, that the analysis, which reveals those factors affecting the economic viability of a Yukon aluminum smelter and the uncertainties in future prospects for the industry, together with the approximate estimates of maximum electric energy costs, constitute a valuable contribution to the knowledge required for informed electric power policy development in the Yukon.

The Westwater Research Centre recognizes fully that other factors besides the cost of electric power enter into a determination of whether an aluminum smelter is appropriate for the Yukon. On the one hand the government could decide to promote the development of a smelter by offering to subsidize the price of power. Alternatively, it could conclude that the environmental and social effects would make a smelter an undesirable development. Nevertheless, there seems to be little doubt that the price for power necessary to make a smelter viable in comparison with the actual cost of such a block of power would be an important consideration. We believe, therefore, that this study, which estimates what the approximate price that electric power will need to be in order to make an aluminum smelter viable, is a valuable contribution to policy development.

This study is one of several that are being undertaken by the Westwater Research Centre as part of a program of studies dealing with water resources management in the Yukon. The program was launched with the financial assistance of the Canadian Arctic Resources Committee. This particular study was supported from a grant provided by the Donner Canadian Foundation.

Irving K. Fox
Professor
Westwater Research Centre
and Director of the Yukon Water
Resources Project

TABLE OF CONTENTS

TABLE OF CONTENTS (Continued)

TABLE OF CONTENTS (Continued)

LIST OF TABLES

LIST OF TABLES (Continued)

LIST OF FIGURES

I   INTRODUCTION

In recent years the hydroelectric power potential of the Yukon has been attracting more and more attention. Engineering studies have identified a number of potential damsites that could generate varying amounts of electric power; further investigations of these sites are underway. With growing pressures to develop some of this hydro potential, decision makers are faced with questions of what size of facility is required and what the eventual cost of this power to the consumers would be. In the case of the Yukon, however, the answers to these questions present an impasse to hydro development. Current electrical demands are too small to justify a large hydro project that could generate power at a relatively low cost, but the power produced from a Yukon-sized hydro plant would be significantly more expensive to consumers.

One of the ways suggested to overcome this dilemma is to invite energy intensive industry to participate in the development of hydroelectric power. Such industries would provide the load necessary to justify a larger power plant and, in turn, other consumers of electricity would benefit from lower power costs. In addition, such industries would add employment and income benefits to the regional economy.

At first glance, this conceptual solution seems practicable. To implement such a solution, however, requires a great deal of information and study. It is necessary to first identify which industries would be appropriate, and then evaluate whether such industries could actually operate in the Yukon and remain competitive in the world market place. The results of such studies would then indicate to decision-makers whether or not to pursue industrial development in the Yukon as a prerequisite to hydroelectric development.

The purpose of this study is to determine whether an aluminum smelter could be part of an overall industrial development plan leading to construction of a major hydroelectric project. Aluminum smelting is a very energy intensive industry, and would provide the necessary electrical load to justify a large generating facility. However, it is necessary to consider whether the Yukon is a suitable location for a viable smelter operation and what economic conditions must prevail if such a smelter is to remain viable.

This analysis assesses the potential viability of a Yukon aluminum smelter from two perspectives. In Chapter II the role of a Yukon smelter vis-a-vis the world aluminum industry is examined. The current structure of the world industry is described with particular attention to differences between aluminum consuming and producing countries, and the unique corporate structure of the industry. Recent world aluminum demand and supply trends are also identified and a short term world demand/supply forecast is presented. With this background information, it is then possible to determine which markets a Yukon smelter might penetrate and where competing smelters would be located. Potential drawbacks for development of the smelter are also identified. Included in this chapter is a description of the aluminum production process and the materials required for aluminum production.

Chapter III examines the economics of a hypothetical smelter to be developed in the Yukon. Both capital and operating costs of a 170,000 tonne per year smelter are identified, along with an estimate of smelter revenues. This analysis allows calculations of the range of electrical power costs under which a smelter could operate and remain competitive in the world market. These electrical power costs represent the main criterion for determining whether or not an aluminum smelter would be a viable industry in the Yukon.

A summary of the results of the analysis is presented in Chapter IV. Both the macro-economic and micro-economic aspects of smelter development in the Yukon are discussed with the intent to enable decision-makers to determine whether or not an aluminum smelter should be included as part of strategy leading to the development of hydroelectric power in the Yukon.

II   OVERVIEW OF THE WORLD ALUMINUM INDUSTRY

The purpose of this chapter is to provide some of the technical and economic knowledge necessary to evaluate the potential for developing an aluminum smelter in the Yukon Territory. By reviewing the technical process for aluminum production, the raw materials requirements, and the structure of the world aluminum industry, those factors of relevance to the establishment of a smelter in the Yukon will be identified.

1.0   THE PRODUCTION PROCESS

Although aluminum is the most abundant metallic element in the earth's crust, it occurs in nature only as part of chemical compounds, mainly oxides and silicates. To produce aluminum metal requires substantial processing of aluminum ores. Processing is a three stage process which starts with the mining of bauxite (aluminum ore). This bauxite is upgraded to produce an intermediate product (alumina) which is in turn reduced through electrolysis to produce aluminum metal. Depending on the efficiency of the processing plants involved, four to six tonnes of bauxite are required to produce two tonnes of alumina which is then reduced to one tonne of aluminum. A detailed description of each stage of the production process is provided below.

1.1   Mining and Processing of Bauxite

Bauxite is found throughout the world, with Africa, South America and Australia having the greatest know reserves. In most instances, bauxite deposits are found near the surface so that open pit mining techniques are employed to remove the ore. Recovered ore is then transported to a treatment plant where bauxite is crushed and washed to remove sand and other impurities. Where bauxite ores are transported large distances to alumina processing plants, the ore is also dried to minimize weight and transportation costs.

1.2   Alumina Production

The process for upgrading bauxite to alumina to bauxite was originally patented in 1888 by K. Bayer in Germany. Today, the same general process is still utilized although some modifications have been made to accommodate different types of aluminum ores. The first stage of the process requires mixing the bauxite with a caustic leach solution and then heating the mixture under pressure to produce a sodium aluminate solution. After the solution is cooled, it is then seeded with crystals to precipitate out alumina trihydrate. This alumina trihydrate is filtered, washed and then calcined to produce alumina (aluminum oxide).

1.3   Primary Aluminum Production

Discovery of the electrolysis process which converts alumina to aluminum predates the development of the Bayer process for alumina production. C.M. Hall in the United States and P. Heroult in France simultaneously discovered the electrolysis process in 1886. Again, this process is still used in aluminum smelters operating today.

The electrolysis reaction takes place in a reduction cell or pot (see Figure II-1). These pots are about ten feet wide, 20 feet long and three feet deep, and are lined with carbon which acts as the cathode for the electrolysis reaction. In modern smelters, between 100 and 240 of these cells are joined to form a pot line, and most smelters operate a number of these pot lines.

The anode for the reaction is also made of carbon but is consumed as the reaction continues. Two designs for anodes are currently in use. In the Soderburg design the anode is formed continuously by adding carbon to a hopper suspended above the pot. The heat from the electrical current used and the reaction itself causes the carbon extruding from the hopper to bake and this produces the anode. For the prebake design, a series of prebaked, preformed carbon blocks are supported in the electrolyte in the pot; blocks are replaced individually as they wear out. The prebake system is more energy efficient but requires more labour than the Soderburg anode design.

5

FIGURE II-1

CROSS SECTION OF AN ALUMINUM REDUCTION CELL

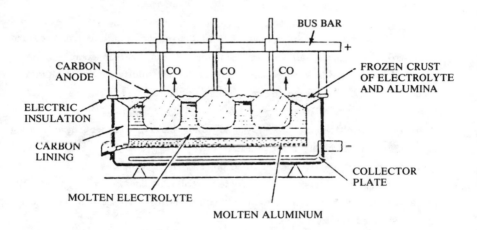

Within each pot is an electrolytic solution called cyrolite; cyrolite is a compound containing sodium, aluminum and fluorine (Na_3AlF_6). Alumina is added to this solution and an electrical current is applied. Each pot uses a direct current of between 65,000 and 150,000 amperes at about five volts. This current passes through the electrolyte and keeps the molten bath at temperatures between 930 and 980°C. In the solution the aluminum metal gradually separates and is removed every one to three days. To keep the process continuous, more alumina is added periodically and more cyrolite and aluminum flouride are added to keep the appropriate balance in the electrolytic solution. Fluorspar (calcium fluoride) is also added to reduce the melting point of the bath. Most pot lines can then operate continuously for three or four years until the carbon lining of the pot is eroded.

The aluminum metal collected from each of the reduction cells is collected and combined, then fluxed, alloyed or cast into ingots. While some aluminum smelters have secondary processing facilities, much of the primary aluminum produced is shipped to processing or fabricating plants.

Overall, the Hall-Heroult process is 85 to 90 percent efficient in producing aluminum from alumina. The process is highly energy intensive and requires a good source of uninterruptible electric power. As fluorine evaporates from the pots during the electrolysis reaction some air pollution does occur. However, the prebake anode system permits efficient collection of offgases and the fluorine can be removed by scrubbing.

2.0 MATERIALS REQUIREMENTS

For the purpose of defining the raw materials required for a Yukon smelter, it is necessary to elaborate on the aluminum processing information described above. In this section those materials necessary for the production of alumina and aluminum will be identified, and the quantities necessary to produce one tonne of aluminum metal will be estimated. The cost of these materials will be estimated later in conjunction with estimating the costs of building and operating an aluminum smelter in the Yukon.

2.1 Alumina Production

The production of alumina is a fairly simple process in terms of the types of materials used. Aside from bauxite, caustic soda is necessary for the leaching process and starch is used to speed the precipitation of alumina trihydrate from the sodium aluminate solution. Upgrading bauxite to alumina does, however, require a considerable amount of energy - an average of about 21.5 gigajoules per tonne of alumina.[1] This energy is primarily supplied by fossil fuels - oil, gas, coal - and is used for heating the leaching solution and for calcining the alumina trihydrate to remove water from the alumina.

Estimates of the quantities of materials needed to produce one tonne of alumina are shown in Table II-1. The figures shown have been adapted from data published by the U.S. Bureau of Mines in 1975. A range of materials requirements per tonne of alumina is shown to indicate the different operating regimes at alumina production plants in the United States, and reflects the different composition of the bauxite ores used at these plants.

In Canada there is only one bauxite processing plant; Alcan's refinery at Jonquiere which produces the alumina used in Alcan's four smelters in Quebec. Based on recent information from Alcan and a report prepared for the Royal Commission on Corporate Concentration[2], the Jonquiere bauxite refinery uses slightly more bauxite per tonne of alumina but substantially less energy; this

TABLE II-1

ESTIMATED QUANTITIES OF RAW MATERIALS
REQUIRED TO PRODUCE ONE TONNE OF ALUMINA

Bauxite		2.0	-	2.2 tonnes

Caustic or equivalent soda ash and lime

Sodium hydroxide	50	-	70	kg.
Lime	20	-	50	kg.
Lime	20	-	50	kg.
Starch	4	-	6	kg.

Energy*

Digester steam (coal, oil, gas)	13	-	16	GJ
Calcining kiln (oil, gas)	4	-	6	GJ
Miscellaneous (coal, oil, gas, electricity)	1	-	3	GJ

Labour (man-hours)	2	-	3

* Excludes energy required to produce lime and caustic soda, estimated at 0.3 to 0.6 GJ and 2.3 to 4.1 GJ, respectively, per tonne of alumina.

SOURCE: Adapted from U.S. Bureau of Mines, 1975. Mineral Facts and Problems.

lower energy use is in part attributable to higher efficiency boilers developed since 1975.

It is interesting to note that, in the past, location of alumina producing plants was based mainly on the availability of fossil fuels and good rail or marine transportation facilities. Recently, however, more and more alumina plants are being built close to bauxite deposits. Such locations save substantially on the volume of materials being transported for processing and cut transportation costs. In addition, those countries having bauxite deposits are becoming more insistent that primary upgrading be done in the country; this provides much needed employment and income benefits in many Third World countries.

2.2 Production of Primary Aluminum

In reducing alumina to aluminum, the most important input to the process, besides alumina, is electric power. Depending on the type of anode used in the smelting process, the electrical requirements necessary to produce aluminum amount to between 50 and 70 gigajoules per tonne of aluminum. The nature of the electrolysis reaction requires that the source of this electric power be either a dedicated electric power plant, such as the one at Kemano for the Kitimat smelters, or uninterruptible power supplied from electric utilities. Any interruption of electricity supply for a period of over 30 minutes can result in freezing of the alumina - cryolite solution in the reduction cells and it may take several months to again reach production if a "freeze-up" does occur.[3] Given the importance of electricity to the aluminum smelting process, the cost of that electricity is a key component in determining the economics of aluminum production.

Another part of aluminum production is the fabrication of the anodes and cathodes in the reduction cells. The materials for both anodes and cathodes is the same, consisting of a combination of petroleum coke, pitch and anthracite coal. This mixture is used to line each reduction cell (pot) and then the coated cell is baked to solidify the carbon layer. Anodes may either be prebaked carbon blocks or be formed continuously during the electrolysis reaction (Soderburg process). For each type of anode, the carbon materials used in their manufacture are substantially the same. However, external baking of the prebaked anodes requires a substantially higher energy input for the Soderburg anodes; this energy may be in the form of oil, gas, or electricity. As the Soderburg anodes are baked as part of the electrolysis reaction, the electrolysis reaction requires additional electric power inputs. These differences in energy inputs can be estimated from Table II-2 which estimates the quantities of materials used to produce a tonne of aluminum using each of the different anode types.

The electrolyte in each reduction cell consists of cryolite, usually synthetic, with aluminum fluoride and calcium fluoride being periodically added to the cell to maintain the fluoride concentration in the solution. During the process, fluorine is absorbed by the pot lining and also dissipates into the atmosphere as fluorine gas. Much of the fluorine can be recovered from offgases and is recycled into the cells.

Once the aluminum is separated from the electrolytic solution, additional energy is required to keep the aluminum molten, to cast ingots, and to alloy the aluminum with other metals. The amount of energy required for these operations is relatively small (only 6 - 9 GJ) compared to other parts of the smelting process. Again, this energy can be supplied by using either fossil fuels or electricity.

The raw materials requirements shown in Table II-2 were based on figures prepared by the U.S. Bureau of Mines in 1975. These estimates are very similar to the raw materials requirements for the Alcan smelters in Canada, although in terms of electrical energy inputs, Alcan is more efficient than many of the plants characterized in Table II-2.[4] Alcan uses both the prebaked and Soderburg anodes in its Canadian smelter operations, but is using prebaked anodes in new plants and for replacement of anodes in existing smelters because of the higher efficiency and reduced environmental impacts of the prebake system.

TABLE II-2

ESTIMATED QUANTITIES OF RAW MATERIALS REQUIRED TO PRODUCE ONE TONNE OF PRIMARY ALUMINUM METAL

	Prebaked		Type of Anode	Soderburg	
Alumina	1900 - 1950	kg.		1900 - 1950	
Electrolyte					
Cryolite	5 - 35	kg.		5 - 35	
Aluminum Fluoride	13 - 30	kg.		13 - 30	
Calcium Fluoride	2 - 4	kg.		2 - 4	
Anode and Cathode					
Petroleum Coke	350 - 475	kg.		350 - 400	
Pitch	140 - 165	kg.		140 - 165	
Anthracite Coal	20 - 30	kg.		30 - 40	
Energy*					
Alumina reduction (electricity)	52 - 65	GJ		64 - 70	
Anode and Cathode baking (oil, gas, electricity)	3 - 6	GJ		0.1 - 0.2	
Holding furnace, ingot casting and melting operations (oil, gas, electricity)	6 - 9	GJ		6 - 9	
Labour (man-hours)	9 - 17			11 - 22	

* Excludes energy required to produce fluorine compounds, estimated at 2-8 GJ per tonne of aluminum metal, and to calcine petroleum coke, equivalent to 1-2 GJ per tonne.

SOURCE: Adapted from U.S. Bureau of Mines, 1975. Mineral Facts and Problems.

Given the amount of electricity used to produce aluminum and the rising costs of electric power, research is underway to make the smelting process more efficient. Most of this research is directed toward finding ways to reduce the electric resistance of anode, cathode and electrolyte; the resistance of these materials under current technology produces considerable heat and wastes 60 to 70 percent of the electrical energy applied to the reduction cells. The results of this research are already in evidence. A recent report by the Battelle Memorial Institute[5] notes a 1979 U.S. Department of Commerce study that suggests new aluminum smelters (as of 1976) would require only 51 GJ per tonne of aluminum. Such consumption represents a 15 percent improvement over current consumption in the Alcan smelters.

Recent improvements in smelting efficiency have been introduced by the Sumitomo Chemical Company. These improvements include lined electrodes, closer electrode spacing, improved insulation and computer control. In 1978 Sumitomo was licensing the use of this technology which was reported to cut electricity consumption to 48 GJ per tonne of aluminum produced. This represents a 20 percent improvement over current Alcan consumption and is considered to represent a 25 percent reduction in average smelter electrical requirements.

In the United States, ALCOA has been experimenting with the use of a chloride bath (as opposed to a fluoride bath). This process was initially reported to operate at lower temperatures, reduce pollution and use 30 percent less energy than the conventional smelting process. Such a reduction would cut power consumption to only 44 GJ per tonne and would represent a 27 percent improvement over current Alcan consumption. In a recent journal[6], however, the chlorine-based process is said to have run into serious corrosion problems. Despite such problems, ALCOA is converting part of a smelter in Texas to further evaluate the technological success of the new process. Redesign, construction and operation of the smelter is expected to take three or four years; commercial operation of the smelter may be possible by 1987.

2.3   Summary of Material Requirements

A summary of the main types and quantities of materials necessary to produce one tonne of aluminum is shown in Figure II-2. Implicit in this figure are a number of assumptions.   It was assumed that new smelter facilities will use prebaked anodes for better energy efficiency and will adopt the best current reduction technology - that of the Sumitomo Chemical Company.   Also, fossil fuels were assumed to be used for prebaking of the anodes and cathodes for reasons of better efficiency and ease of process control. The quantities shown are based on interpretation of the most reliable data from the U.S. Bureau of Mines, the U.S. Department of Commerce and the Battelle Memorial Institute.

The diagram suggests an integrated alumina production facility and aluminum smelter. While some such integrated facilities do exist, it is now more common for aluminum smelters to import alumina from other areas. (This is discussed more fully in the next section). Depending on the relative locations of bauxite reserves, the alumina reduction plant, and the aluminum smelter, transportation may be a major factor not included in Figure II-2. While not a raw material input, transportation never-the-less warrants special consideration and will be discussed in detail in the analysis of the potential for a Yukon Smelter.

The materials and quantities shown in Figure II-2 will form the basis for assessing the economic cost of producing aluminum in the Yukon. That section of the report will also consider the capital requirements for a smelter, the workforce, and the infrastructure necessary to make a smelter operable.

FIGURE II-2

MATERIALS REQUIRED TO PRODUCE ONE TONNE OF
ALUMINUM IN A MODERN INTEGRATED SMELTER OPERATION

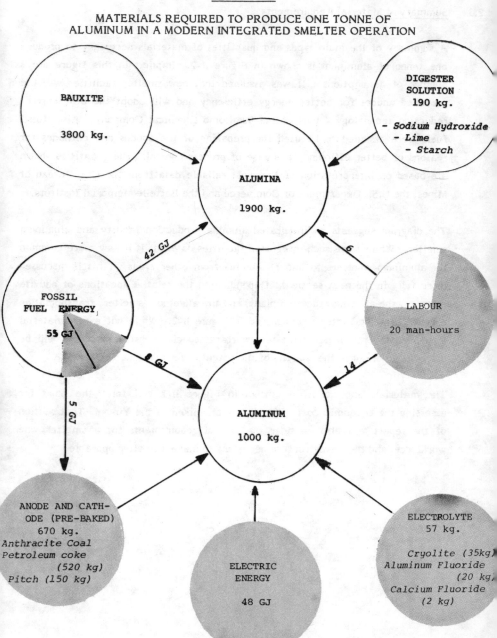

BAUXITE

3800 kg.

DIGESTER
SOLUTION
190 kg.

- *Sodium Hydroxide*
- *Lime*
- *Starch*

ALUMINA

1900 kg.

FOSSIL
FUEL ENERGY

55 GJ

42 GJ

6

LABOUR

20 man-hours

8 GJ

14

5 GJ

ALUMINUM

1000 kg.

ANODE AND CATH-
ODE (PRE-BAKED)
670 kg.
*Anthracite Coal
Petroleum coke
          (520 kg)
Pitch (150 kg)*

ELECTRIC
ENERGY

48 GJ

ELECTROLYTE
57 kg.

*Cryolite (35kg)
Aluminum Fluoride
          (20 kg)
Calcium Fluoride
          (2 kg)*

3.0 INDUSTRY STRUCTURE

Of direct relevance to this study is the structure of the aluminum industry. A variety of factors determine where smelters can be built, and by examining the location of existing smelter operations it is possible to identify those factors and their relative importance in determining smelter location. Such information is of considerable importance in determining whether or not the Yukon is an appropriate location to build a smelter.

In examining industry structure two different perspectives will be used. First, the geographical and political distribution of bauxite reserves, alumina plants and aluminum smelters will be considered. The present distribution clearly shows major differences between raw material sources and aluminum producing countries. Major changes in this distribution are expected in the near future. Any such changes will have important ramifications for a Yukon smelter site. Such an analysis will also suggest what sources of bauxite or alumina are likely to be used by a Yukon aluminum smelter.

The second perspective for examining the aluminum industry is that of the corporate structure of the industry. A majority of alumina and aluminum producing plants are owned to varying degrees by a few very large companies. An oligopolistic situation has resulted and this affects the economics of aluminum production. The impact of this oligopoly on smelter location and operation must be detailed in order to assess the feasibility of an aluminum smelter in the Yukon.

3.1 Sources of Bauxite

Bauxite is found throughout much of the world although the actual composition of the ore varies from deposit to deposit. Most of the principal commercial deposits are located in less developed countries in Central and South America, Africa and Oceania. .Development of these deposits has historically been undertaken by major aluminum producing companies whose smelters are located in North America, Europe and Japan.

Almost 75 million tonnes of bauxite were produced in the western world in 1979. This output was slightly higher than production in previous years. The largest world producer of bauxite is Australia, with 1979 production totalling about 26 million tonnes. Other significant bauxite producing companies are listed in Table II-3 and include Guinea, Jamaica, Surinam and Guyana. Aside from Australia, most bauxite production is concentrated in Central America and Africa, which together accounted for another 26 million tonnes or 35 percent of bauxite production in the western world.

No shortage of bauxite is foreseen in the future. In their 1975 report, the U.S. Bureau of Mines note that known world reserves of bauxite are adequate to meet world demand beyond the year 2000. A more recent report in Mining Annual Review claims that bauxite reserves in Guyana are very much larger than previously assumed. In addition, new technologies are being developed to extract alumina from ores thought to be uneconomical under existing technologies. Thus, availability of bauxite is not a major obstacle for the development of new alumina processing facilities.

3.2   Alumina Processing Plants

During the early development of the aluminum industry, alumina processing plants were located near inexpensive power sources or close to the markets for primary aluminum products. As countries in Central and South America and Africa then lacked the necessary energy resources, bauxite was shipped to countries such as the United States, West Germany, Japan, U.S.S.R. and Canada for upgrading to alumina. On a smaller scale, some countries with indigenous bauxite resources also developed upgrading facilities; such countries include Greece, Turkey, Yugoslavia, Australia and India.

With the increase in energy costs during the early 1970's, it became progressively more expensive to ship a large volume, low-cost commodity like bauxite over great distances for processing. To avoid these higher transport costs, the major aluminum companies invested in bauxite upgrading facilities nearer the bauxite reserves, and often had to develop the power sources necessary to run the

TABLE II-3

WESTERN WORLD PRODUCTION OF BAUXITE IN 1979

(thousand tonnes)

Oceania	Australia	26,000	26,000
South America	Brazil	1,400	
	Guyana	3,000	9,400
	Surinam	5,000	
Central America	Jamaica	12,000	
	Dominican Republic	540	13,140
	Haiti	600	
North American	United States	1,700	1,700
Africa	Guinea	12,000	
	Sierra Leone	700	13,000
	Ghana	300	
Asia	India	2,100	
	Malaysia	300	
	Indonesia	1,010	3,560
	Turkey	150	
Europe	Yugoslavia	2,900	
	Greece	2,720	7,660
	France	2,040	
TOTAL			74,460

facilities. By 1974 half of the bauxite produced was being upgraded to alumina in the country of origin. Since then, most new alumina plants have been constructed in those countries having bauxite resources and a relatively stable political climate.

Exact world capacity for producing alumina at this time is not known. A recent journal[7] indicated that Australia, with a capacity of 7.2 million tonnes per year in 1980, was now the major alumina producer in the world, accounting for about 25 percent of the world's production capacity. This would suggest world capacity at about 30 million tonnes of alumina per year in 1980.

A survey of potential new alumina processing plants was prepared in 1980[8], and suggests that most new alumina plants under construction or in the planning stages would be built in bauxite producing countries. Alumina production capacity is expected to increase by 1.5 to 2 million tonnes annually over the next five years. Much of this increased capacity (2.3 million tonnes per year) will be built in Australia but other large alumina plants are scheduled for Venezuela (1.0 million tonnes), Brazil (0.8 million tonnes), Eire (0.8 million tonnes), Jamaica (0.6 million tonnes) and Italy (0.5 million tonnes). By 1985, alumina production is expected to be about 37 million tonnes per year, a 19 percent increase over existing capacity. In addition, the report speculated on a number of other new plants that would add another seven million tonnes of alumina production capacity. Much of this potential would be developed in Australia but the timing of construction and operation of such plants has not yet been defined.

3.3   Aluminum Smelters

Location of aluminum smelters is dependent on two main factors: a reliable source of inexpensive electric power and good transportation access to bauxite or alumina sources. Historically, the necessary transportation and power infrastructures were available only in the more developed countries and so most aluminum smelting capacity now exists in North America, Europe and Japan. A list of aluminum producing countries and their production in 1979 is presented in Table II-4.

TABLE II-4

WESTERN WORLD PRODUCTION OF ALUMINUM IN 1979

(thousands of tonnes)

N. AMERICA	U.S.A.	4557	S. AMERICA	Brazil	239
	Canada	863		Venezuela	207
	Mexico	43		Argentina	123
		5463		Surinam	58
					627
EUROPE	W. Germany	742	ASIA	Japan	1010
	Norway	673		India	209
	France	395		Bahrain	126
	U.K.	360		Turkey	30
	Italy	269		S. Korea	18
	Spain	258		Iran	5
	Netherlands	255			1398
	Yugoslavia	180			
	Greece	141			
	Austria	93	AFRICA	Ghana	166
	Switzerland	83		Egypt	104
	Iceland	72		South Africa	86
		3604		Cameroon	45
					401
OCEANIA	Australia	272			
	New Zealand	153			
		425			

It is noteworthy that little aluminum smelting capacity exists in those countries in Central America, South America and Africa which have bauxite deposits. Even Australia, which has the largest known bauxite reserves plays a small role in world aluminum production. Due to the way in which the aluminum industry has evolved there is now a major distinction between those countries that produce aluminum, and those countries that produce bauxite. This distinction is clearly shown in Table II-5 which shows that North America and Europe accounted for over 76 percent of the aluminum produced in the western world in 1979 but only 12 percent of the world's bauxite. In contrast, countries in Central America, Oceania, and Africa produced 70 percent of the bauxite mined in 1979 but smelted only seven percent of the aluminum produced that year. This current imbalance is expected to change gradually as industrial development proceeds in the bauxite producing countries.

Within the aluminum producing countries, smelters are centred in areas of former and recent low cost power. In the United States, for instance, smelters are located in the Pacific Northwest, the Tennessee, Ohio and St. Lawrence Valleys, and North Carolina, where power is supplied by such agencies as the Bonneville Power Administration and the Tennessee Valley Authority. In Canada, Kitimat was chosen as a smelter site due to the low-cost hydrolectric potential at nearby Kemano.

As the availability of electric power is the principal determinant of locating new smelters, the future of many existing smelters also relies on the cost and continued availability of electricity. In recent years, many smelters have either had to close or cut back production because of increasing energy costs. This is particularly true where electricity is produced in oil or gas-fired power plants. For example, in Japan prior to 1978, oil-fired plants accounted for 72 percent of the electricity required by smelters. To accommodate higher oil prices, the government reduced production to 58 percent of capacity, scrapped 275 thousand tonnes of capacity and froze an additional 255 thousand tonnes of capacity. Although the reduced production and frozen capacity was to last only five years, it is questionable as to whether the oil-supply situation will have improved sufficiently to warrant reopening these smelters.

TABLE II-5

COMPARISON OF ALUMINUM AND BAUXITE PRODUCTION BY CONTINENT, 1979

(Excludes Communist Bloc Countries)

	Bauxite Production		Aluminum Production			
	Million Tonnes	% of Total	Million Tonnes	% of Total	Capacity Million Tonnes	Utilization of Capacity
North America	1.7	2.3	5.5	46.2	5.8	94.8%
Central America	13.1	17.6	---	---	---	---
South America	9.4	12.6	0.6	5.0	0.7	86.6%
Europe	7.6	10.2	3.6	30.3	3.7	97.1%
Asia	3.6	4.8	1.4	11.8	1.7	81.5%
Africa	13.0	17.5	0.4	3.4	0.4	90.5%
Oceania	26.0	34.9	0.4	3.4	0.4	98.8%
Total Western World	74.4		11.9		12.8	93.2%

In some countries smelters powered by electricity from hydroelectric sources are also facing a questionable future. As residential and commercial sector load growth consumes more and more of each hydroelectric plant's output, less electricity is available on a firm basis for industrial users like aluminum smelters. Consequently, power supplies to aluminum smelters are sometimes cut-off during periods of power shortage and this can have disastrous results in the smelters.[9] Power shortages are now occurring in the Pacific Northwest of the U.S., which accommodates one-third of U.S. smelter capacity. This situation was further aggravated in 1979 by water shortages in hydroelectric reservoirs and ten percent of the region's smelter capacity was closed. Such power shortages have also tended to push the cost of electricity higher and higher, thereby increasing the cost of aluminum production and altering the competitiveness of U.S. aluminum on the world market. With long term contracts with the Bonneville Power Administration expiring in the early 1980's, there is some concern for the future of aluminum smelters in the Pacific Northwest. However, increased energy efficiency in the smelting process (see Section 2.2) is expected to alleviate some of the expected energy shortage problems.

In a recent article in the Mining Journal, it was noted that the aluminum industries in several countries, including Japan, the U.S., Taiwan, Great Britain, Turkey and India, were facing energy cost and availability problems.[10] Such problems may cause further closures of smelter capacity and new smelters are expected to be based on thermal power supplies. The article concludes that most new smelter capacity built will be centred in Australia for the following reasons:

- Australia has the largest known reserves of bauxite;

- Australia has enormous supplies of coal close to the bauxite reserves;

- Australia is more politically stable than other countries with good bauxite and energy prospects (Brazil, Guyana and Venezuela); and,

- Australia has a lower rate of inflation than most of its competitors.

A survey of planned and proposed smelter additions throughout the world corroborates this assessment.[11] Australian smelter capacity is expected to grow from 280 thousand tonnes in 1979 to 1.3 million tonnes by 1985. Should this increase in production capacity actually occur, some production capacity in other countries will become uneconomical and may warrant smelter closures. The extent of such closures will ultimately depend on world aluminum demand but Australia is expected to have a tremendous power cost advantage, with power costs being only 33 percent of corresponding costs in the United States.

While Australia is expected to be the location of most new smelter capacity in the 1980's, Brazil and Venezuela are likely to become as important during the 1990's. Both countries are close to bauxite reserves (Brazil has major bauxite reserves in the Amazon Basin) and both have abundant energy resources; Brazil has the hydroelectric potential of the Amazon River while Venezuela has oil and gas reserves.

The trend that appears in the above discussion is that most new smelter capacity will be built in those countries which have potential for abundant energy and indigenous bauxite reserves, while existing smelters in North America, Europe and Japan will gradually decline as production costs increase and power shortages occur. Thus, the current distinction between bauxite-producing countries and aluminum-producing as shown in Table II-5 will be less noticeable during the next decade. A discussion of what changes in aluminum production will occur in the short run is contained in Section 4.0 which presents a world aluminum supply/demand forecast to 1985.

3.4 Corporate Structure of the Industry

The world aluminum industry has a unique corporate structure in that six large firms have equity interests in half of the world's alumina and aluminum production capacity. These firms are integrated, multi-national corporations with diverse holdings throughout the world, and include the following:

Alcan Aluminium Ltd. (Alcan)
Aluminum Company of America (ALCOA)
Reynolds Metals Company
Kaiser Aluminum and Chemical Corp.
Pechiney Ugine Kuhlmann Group (PUK)
Swiss Aluminium Ltd. (Alusuisse)

In addition to holding half of the world's aluminum capacity, these firms also have major investments in bauxite production and in 1975 they owned over 40 percent of the world's bauxite production capacity. This vertically integrated structure allows each firm to transfer raw materials (bauxite and alumina included) from one subsidiary to another at prices below the world market price. Consequently, the aluminum eventually produced by these six companies also enjoys a cost advantage on the world market; the resulting world price for aluminum therefore reflects the concentration of production capacity in six firms. The other advantage held by these six firms is that owing to their size and assets, they are better able to raise the capital required to build more bauxite, alumina and aluminum production facilities. With these advantages, the six companies are expected to continue to play a major role in developing bauxite reserves and adding new smelter capacity.

To illustrate the diversity and magnitude of holdings by these six large firms, the case of Alcan Aluminium Ltd. is considered here. Alcan is probably best known for its Canadian smelters and alumina plant. In Quebec, Alcan operates four smelters which utilize alumina produced by their alumina plant at Jonquiere, P.Q. The bauxite used at this alumina plant is from Jamalcan in Jamaica; Jamalcan is a joint venture between Alcan (93 percent of assets) and the Jamaican Government (seven percent of assets). The other Alcan smelter at Kitimat is supplied with alumina produced in Australia by Alcan Australia. Alcan has additional smelters in Brazil, West Germany (Alcan Aluminiumwerke), and the United Kingdom. Alcan also participates as a partner in other smelters, including the Endasa smelter in Spain (20.5 percent Alcan) and three smelters owned by the Indian Aluminum Co. (55 percent Alcan). Alcan recently sold its 25 percent interest in Ardal og Sunndal in Norway although Alcan will continue to supply the smelters with alumina and to purchase ingots. Alcan is also participating in many projects currently under construction or being planned. These projects include a new smelter at Grand Baie (Quebec), a new bauxite mine in Brazil near Trombetas as part of a consortium, an alumina plant in Eire (40 percent Alcan), further expansion of the Kurri Kurri smelter in Australia, and a new smelter to be built in conjunction with Queensland Alumina Ltd. in Australia. While these holdings are diverse and clearly show the inter-relationship between bauxite and aluminum production, Alcan also has many subsidiaries in the aluminum fabrication industry in more than 30 countries throughout the world.

In addition to the six large firms described above, about forty other firms account for another 25 percent of world aluminum production capacity. These firms typically participate at only one level of the bauxite to aluminum production process and may be associated with one of the six larger firms or with governments.

The remaining 25 percent of production capacity is owned in whole or in part by governments of countries having indigenous bauxite reserves and wishing to participate in local upgrading to alumina or aluminum. Examples of such countries include Guyana, Jamaica, Surinam, Brazil, Turkey, Indonesia, the Philippines, India, Bahrain, Dubai, Egypt and Guinea. In these instances, governments can assist financing of new projects (through bond issues), provide tax incentives, and help develop the infrastructure (power and transportaion) necessary to produce aluminum for the world market. As more and more aluminum production capacity is to be built in bauxite producing countries, more and more government participation in new projects is anticipated. For companies wishing to invest in such new projects, political stability will become an important investment criterion.

3.5   Implications for a Yukon Smelter

To be viable, a Yukon aluminum smelter would have to be compatible with the current or projected structure of the world aluminum industry. In the review of current industry structure, a number of critical locational and operational factors were noted. This section examines those factors and considers whether a Yukon smelter would fit into the general pattern of development of the world aluminum industry.

First, the Yukon would be a very poor site for an alumina plant. Bauxite supplies are very distant and it would not be economical to import such a low-cost, high volume raw material. In addition, most bauxite producing countries are attempting to develop their own alumina plants and would probably be averse to exporting a large quantity of bauxite to new upgrading plants in the Yukon. For these reasons, a Yukon smelter should import alumina and should not include a bauxite upgrading facility.

Second, a review of new and planned aluminum smelters indicates a tendency to locate smelters in areas close to bauxite or alumina sources and inexpensive electric power. A Yukon smelter would be no where near most current or planned alumina production facilities and would also be a considerable distance from recognized aluminum markets in Japan, Canada and the United States. Due to the distances involved, transportation costs for raw materials and finished products may push the price of aluminum from a Yukon smelter above world aluminum prices. However, high transportation costs may be offset if the cost of electricity is sufficiently low to push Yukon production costs below world production costs.

A third consideration is that it may be difficult to obtain the supply of alumina necessary to operate a Yukon smelter. Alumina exporting countries are now trying to promote the development of indigenous smelter capacity and would be averse to supplying alumina to a competing smelter operation in another country. This situation is particularly true for a Yukon smelter because Australia is the closest source of alumina. Although Australia would honour long term alumina supply contracts with current smelter operations, much of the planned expansion of Australian smelting capacity is predicated on domestic bauxite and alumina supplies. Additional exports of alumina might therefore adversely affect the planned expansions in Australia and would not be favoured.

One way of perhaps avoiding this alumina supply problem would be to have one of the six large aluminum producing companies with alumina production capacity in Australia participate in smelter development. Such a solution would have other benefits for aluminum production. As an affiliate or subsidiary of a firm like Alcan, a Yukon smelter might be able to purchase other raw materials at transfer prices, not world prices, and would benefit from lower aluminum production costs. As a subsidiary, a Yukon smelter would also benefit from the parent company's management experience and their knowledge of product markets. Such a corporate structure would definitely enhance the feasibility of a Yukon smelter and help assure its financial viability.

4.0   SUPPLY/DEMAND RELATIONSHIPS

To help determine whether an aluminum smelter in the Yukon would be economic, it is necessary to examine world aluminum supply/demand relationships to see if markets would exist for Yukon aluminum production. In this section, an analysis of aluminum supply and demand over the last decade is presented to indicate what factors affect supply/demand and to determine recent growth rates. Based on this historical data, and forecasts from other published sources, an aluminum supply/demand forecast is developed for the period from 1980 to 1990. The results of this forecast then form the basis for ascertaining the potential marketability of Yukon aluminum. In this assessment particular attention is paid to supply/demand balances in those countries where Yukon aluminum would most likely be marketed.

4.1   World Demand for Aluminum

World demand for primary aluminum, as indicated by aluminum consumption, increased to 12.5 million tonnes in 1979. The United States was the largest single consumer of primary aluminum, accounting for about 40 percent of demand in the western world. Despite its reduced smelter capacity, Japan continues to be the second largest consumer of aluminum. Canadian consumption of aluminum is by comparison relatively small - about three percent of the world's aluminum demand.

Primary aluminum, generally in the form of ingots produced at the smelters, is in demand for a variety of purposes. Most primary aluminum is processed into aluminum plate, sheet, foil, wire, tubes, rods and other wrought products. Much of the remaining aluminum is used in castings. Only small quantities of aluminum are shipped as flakes, powder or paste for further upgrading. In both Canada and the U.S., a similar proportion of aluminum goes to each of the three major end uses:[12]

	U.S.	Canada
Wrought Products	83.3%	84.1%
Castings	15.7%	11.9%
Powder, Paste	1.0%	4.0%

It must be added that while the U.S. imports much of the primary aluminum it uses, Canada is a net exporter of aluminum and consumes only about one-third of the aluminum it produces.

Historically, world consumption of primary aluminum shows cyclical variations that parallel fluctuations in the world economic cycle. Such variation is illustrated by the data in Table II-6 which shows aluminum consumption in the western world between 1973 and 1978. The sudden drop in aluminum consumption in 1975 coincided with the general economic recession experienced throughout the world. Typically, these changes in demand lag behind general economic conditions, so that demands for aluminum increased only after world economic conditions improved in 1976 and 1977.

If aluminum consumption figures were available for 1980, a second downturn in demand would be noted. This decline is also attributable to a general economic recession, and is due particularly to the impact of high interest rates on housing and automobile markets in North America. Expectations are that aluminum consumption in 1980 will have decreased to about 11.8 million tonnes - a drop of about six percent over 1979 levels. Further declines in consumption are expected until such time as world economic conditions improve.

A number of short term forecasts of world aluminum demand have recently been prepared.[13] One forecast prepared by Anthony Bird Associates of Surrey, U.K., suggests that improved economic conditions by 1982/83 should promote large annual increases in aluminum consumption, perhaps as high as ten percent per year. In the meantime, however, consumption in the U.S. is expected to decrease by as much as 13 percent until economic recovery occurs. Metals and Mineral Research Services Ltd. also expects aluminum consumption to decrease in the short term: a five percent decline in 1980 and a two percent decline in

TABLE II-6

WESTERN WORLD CONSUMPTION OF PRIMARY ALUMINUM, 1973 - 1979

(million tonnes)

	1973	1974	1975	1976	1977	1978*
North America	5.4	5.6	3.6	4.8	5.1	5.4
South America	0.3	0.3	0.3	0.3	0.4	0.4
Europe	3.2	3.4	2.8	3.5	3.5	3.6
Asia	2.0	1.7	1.6	2.1	2.0	2.3
Africa	0.1	0.1	0.1	0.1	0.1	0.1
Oceania	0.2	0.2	0.2	0.2	0.2	0.2
Total	11.2	11.3	8.6	9.0	11.3	12.0

* Estimated from information provided by the Department of Energy, Mines and Resources as part of an annual review of the Canadian Minerals industry in 1979.

SOURCE: Metal Statistics 1979, American Metal Market, Fairchild Publications.

1981. Aluminum consumption is then predicted to begin to increase as the world economy enters a growth cycle.

Representatives of the aluminum industry seem to have ignored the potential for a short term decline in aluminum consumption. Kaiser Aluminum and Chemical Corp. recently forecast aluminum consumption to grow by four to six percent throughout the 1980's, based on expectations that the U.S., Western Europe and Japan will experience real economic growth of three to four percent per year over the next decade.[14] Similarly, Alcan Aluminium Ltd. predicts annual average growth of four to five percent in world demand for primary aluminum.[15]

These growth rates concur with the expectations of some earlier demand forecasts. In a forecast prepared in 1975 by the U.S. Bureau of Mines, the demand for primary aluminum was expected to grow at an annual rate of 5.4 percent between 1973 and 1985, and by about 4.8 percent per year between 1985 and 2000[16]. While this forecast did not foresee the short term recessions in the world economy during 1974-75 and 1980, the average rate of growth predicted corresponds closely with the results of recent forecasts, and only slightly over estimates actual world demand for 1979. One of the main arguments behind this forecast was that increasing energy costs would make aluminum more desirable in end uses like transportation equipment and machinery. This prediction has in fact occurred - from model year 1978 to 1979 average aluminum use in automobiles increased by about ten percent to 127 pounds per car - and even more use of aluminum in vehicles is expected in the future.[17]

A second assumption in the forecast by the U.S. Bureau of Mines was that U.S. demand for aluminum would grow more slowly than world demand, for the reason that less developed countries in Africa, Asia and South America would be rapidly expanding their industrial base. This trend now seems to be occurring as the bauxite producing countries are increasing their aluminum production capacity and expanding aluminum processing facilities. Future expansion of the industrial base in these countries will continue to increase world aluminum demand at a faster pace than U.S. demand. In the Bureau of Mines forecast, the aluminum demand growth rates for the U.S. and the rest of the world were as follows:

	1973-1985	1985-2000	1973-2000
U.S. demand	4.9%	4.4%	4.6%
Rest of world demand	5.7%	5.0%	5.3%
World demand	5.4%	4.8%	5.1%

These growth rates suggest that world demand for aluminum should exceed U.S. demand growth by about 0.5 percent annually.

All the demand forecasts cited above clearly agree that world aluminum demand will continue to grow through the 1980's and beyond. And, excluding short term drops in demand associated with world economic conditions, all forecasts agree that demand should increase at rates between four and six percent per year for the next decade. For the purposes of this study, then, world consumption is assumed to increase by four percent per year until 1990, from a starting point of about 11.8 million tonnes in 1980. This growth rate was the most commonly cited and reflects the uncertainty as to how long the current economic recession and high interest rates will remain in North America. Under this assumption, world consumption should increase to about 14.4 million tonnes by 1985 and to 17.5 million tonnes in 1990.

With respect to the United States, the largest aluminum consumer, a world aluminum demand increase of four percent per year implicitly assumes that U.S. consumption would only increase by about 3.5 percent per year and that U.S. GNP would be increasing by only two to three percent. Such growth rates for U.S. aluminum demand are substantially below those rates forecast in 1978 and 1979 by the Bureau of Mines and the Federal Preparedness Agency[18], but at that time no one had envisioned the sudden increase in interest rates and resulting cutbacks in consumer spending. A U.S. aluminum demand study prepared by Charles Rivers Associates in 1977[19], however, estimated aluminum consumption to increase by 3.6 percent per year between 1980 and 1990; this is consistent with the implicit U.S. demand growth assumed here.

4.2 World Supply of Aluminum

The current status of the world supply of aluminum has already been detailed in Section 3.3. For 1979 it was estimated that smelter capacity in the western world amounted to 12.8 million tonnes. From this capacity about 11.9 million tonnes of aluminum were actually produced; this represents a utilization of capacity of 93.2 percent. Presently most smelter capacity is located in North America and Europe where capacity utilization was higher than average. In constrast, aluminum smelters in Asia worked to only 80 percent of capacity, due to power supply problems in India and Japan.

The amount of aluminum produced in any given year is directly related to demand for aluminum in preceding time periods. As aluminum demand has been observed to rise and fall in conjunction with changing economic conditions, aluminum supplies have also varied from year to year. Table II-7 illustrates some of the recent variations in world aluminum demand/supply balances. The impact of the 1975-76 recession clearly indicates a large cutback in aluminum demand with suppliers being slow to react and over producing in those two years. Aluminum demand has risen steadily since 1976, and aluminum suppliers have steadily increased their output and capacity but have been unable to meet world demands without reducing their inventories. These circumstances have created a situation in which the short supply of aluminum in recent years has pushed aluminum prices steadily upwards.

The impact of the current recession in North America on aluminum demand does not show on Table II-7 as figures are not yet available. However, as consumption was estimated to have declined to 11.8 million tonnes, it is estimated that a small surplus of aluminum was produced in 1980 and inventories will once again begin to grow.

Aluminum suppliers respond to changing demands in three different ways. First, when demand begins to fall, suppliers can shut down one or two pot lines and reduce production. Thus, a drop in the utilization of smelter capacity is usually

TABLE II-7

ALUMINUM DEMAND/SUPPLY BALANCES IN THE WESTERN WORLD
1973 - 1979

(million of tonnes)

	Demand	Supply	Balance
1973	11.2	10.1	-1.1
1974	11.3	11.1	-0.2
1975	8.6	9.9	+1.3
1976	9.0	10.2	+1.2
1977	11.3	11.2	-0.1
1978	12.0	11.6	-0.4
1979	12.5	11.9	-0.6

SOURCE: Demand - Table II-6.
         Supply - Mining Annual Review, 1976-1980.

associated with reduced demand. In 1976, for example, only 80 percent of world smelter capacity was in use; this compares to 93 percent in 1979. Given the likelihood that demand for aluminum will fall during the early 1980's, one market analysis firm has suggested that capacity utilization rates will fall to 85 percent by the third quarter of 1981.[20]

The second response of aluminum suppliers is to reduce inventories when demand can no longer be met by smelter production. Under normal conditions, the world aluminum industry maintains an inventory of about two million tonnes - two months supply. In 1979, inventories were decreased by about 0.6 million tonnes in order to satisfy world aluminum demands. Serious depletion of these inventories over an extended period suggests future shortages, and suppliers usually respond by investing in additional capacity. The supply/demand balances of 1977-1979 have initiated the investment cycle underway now, but it is feared that the decline in demand in 1980 will result in inventories being enlarged. Excess production of 1.4 million tonnes between mid-1980 and mid-1981 is expected by one aluminum market analyst.[21]

While factors of capacity utilization and inventory reduction can be successfully used to handle short term variations in demand, suppliers must eventually rely on installing new capacity to accommodate long term increases in demand, such as observed during the last decade. One incentive to undertake such investments is the existence of tight markets and diminishing inventories. A second incentive is that some existing smelter capacity is no longer economically efficient (due to increasing energy prices) and new capacity is required for replacement. Thus, the industry appears to embark on major investment cycles as conditions warrant, and such a cycle is now underway.

Estimates of new smelter capacity to be added in the next decade vary considerably. One assessment suggested capacity increases of 3.8 percent annually between mid-1980 and mid-1983 and by seven percent per year between 1983 and 1987.[22] Kaiser has suggested that smelter capacity would increase by only 1.7 percent annually between 1980 and 2000.[23] Perhaps the most detailed estimate of future capacity is provided in the Mining Annual Review published each year. This report reviews the status of all new smelters currently under construction and those planned for the near future. The overall results of this review are summarized in Table II-8; these results have been calculated by adding each of the new additions planned in each continent for each year. The overall effect is that aluminum production capacity in the western world is assumed to increase by 4.3 percent annually until 1985. The vast majority of new additions are predicted to occur in Australia, with major increases in South America. Smelter capacity in North America and Europe is expected to grow very slowly. These trends reflect the general move in the aluminum industry to locate new smelters in areas with bauxite sources and low cost power.

This forecast may be considered optimistic. Given the three to five year time period between initiating a project and producing aluminum, most of the capacity increases were planned during the tight markets of the late 1970's. Consequently, it is felt by some analysts that while there are tremendous plans by different countries to build new smelters in cheap energy areas, the question of how many smelters are actually necessary has not been adequately addressed. Despite these assertions, a 4.3 percent annual capacity growth figure is felt to be reasonably accurate. The 1980 Mining Annual Review noted some of the potential smelter projects that have only recently been discarded due to concern about potential over-supply problems. Those projects still noted in the review seem to be imminent. Additions to capacity in the period 1985 to 1990 are expected to grow at about the same rate, particularly given the demand forecast in Section 4.1.

TABLE II-8

PRESENT AND PLANNED ALUMINUM PRODUCTION CAPACITY, 1979 - 1985

	Production Capacity (thousand tonnes)							Annual Rate of Change* %
	1979	1980	1981	1982	1983	1984	1985	
North America	5,763	5,875	6,080	6,155	6,185	6,280	6,365	1.6
South America	724	725	835	1,020	1,100	1,180	1,260	11.7
Europe	3,711	3,740	3,840	3,970	4,070	4,120	4,260	2.6
Asia	1,715	1,780	1,870	1,970	2,045	2,180	2,180	4.1
Africa	443	445	505	505	505	505	505	2.6
Oceania	430	490	500	715	1,135	1,395	1,555	26.0
Total Western World	12,786	13,055	13,630	14,235	15,040	15,660	16,125	4.3

* Calculated between 1980 and 1985.

SOURCE: Mining Annual Review 1980.

4.3 <u>Future World Supply/Demand Balance</u>

By comparing the forecasts of world aluminum demand and supply presented in the preceding sections, it is possible to predict the status of the world aluminum industry for the next decade and evaluate the market potential for a Yukon smelter. In Table II-9 the forecasts of demand and smelter capacity are presented, along with a measure of the capacity utilization required to meet demand. In the short run, the supply/demand balance suggests that the drop in aluminum demand in the early 1980's will again result in over-production by the industry and smelter utilization will drop to about 90 percent of capacity. In the longer term, projected demand and supply are forecast to remain in an equilibrium, with new smelters being added to ensure that total smelter capacity stays ahead of demand. Smelter utilization is expected to remain at about 90 percent throughout the decade.

Although an overall demand/supply balance is predicted for the decade, the demand and supply estimates are rather simplistic. As noted before, world aluminum demand usually experiences unpredictable cyclical fluctuations linked to world economic cycles. Consequently, some cyclical demand variation must be expected between 1980 and 1990; such variation has been purposely ignored by using a constant rate of growth in the demand forecast. It would appear, however, that given the predicted rate of smelter additions, enough aluminum production capacity will exist to accommodate most minor fluctuations. Demand fluctuations would only affect capacity utilization rates and the size of inventories, and would have little impact on the rate of new smelter additions.

As forecast, aluminum markets are likely to be steady during the next decade, although periodic tight market conditions may occur. Steady markets typically give rise to gradual price increases, and such price increases for primary aluminum will affect which smelters operate to full capacity. Those smelters facing continually rising energy prices and operating costs will no doubt experience temporary closures or severe reductions in capacity utilization. Those smelters with continued low cost energy and operating costs will probably

TABLE II-9

WORLD ALUMINUM SUPPLY/DEMAND BALANCE, 1980-1990

(million tonnes)

	Demand	Capacity	Required Capacity Utilization to Meet Demand %
1979*	12.5	12.8	97.7
1980	11.8	13.1	90.1
1981	12.3	13.6	90.4
1982	12.8	14.2	90.1
1983	13.3	15.0	88.7
1984	13.8	15.7	87.9
1985	14.4	16.1	89.4
1986	14.9	16.7	89.2
1987	15.5	17.4	89.1
1988	16.1	18.1	89.0
1987	16.8	18.8	89.4
1990	17.5	19.6	89.3

* Actual.

operate near capacity. And those proposed smelters with the lowest energy costs will be hurried into production while those with higher energy costs are delayed. The net result is that smelter capacity will appear to grow steadily, but the distribution of capacity among producing nations will vary considerably throughout the decade. Production capacity will shift away from Europe, North America and Japan, and will increase steadily in Australia and South America.

In summary, the world aluminum industry is expected to reach a supply/demand equilibrium during the 1980's, with smelter capacity staying ahead of demand. The aluminum market will be steady during this period but a shift in production capacity from North America and Europe to Australia is anticipated.

4.4   The Price of Aluminum

In recent years the price of aluminum has risen sharply. Prior to 1973, aluminum prices remained quite stable, in the range of $0.51 to $0.64 (U.S.) per kilogram. In real dollars, the price of aluminum actually declined during that period. Since 1973, however, the price of aluminum has almost trebled, with the current price (January 1981) now being $1.68 per kilogram. Table II-10 shows the rapid increases in aluminum price since 1973, as represented by prices for ingots of 99.5 percent purity.

One reason behind these changing aluminum prices is the overall aluminum supply/demand balance. As noted earlier, the late 1970's were characterized by a shortage of aluminum on world markets which contributed to pushing aluminum prices up very quickly. Currently this supply/demand picture is changing, with aluminum production predicted to exceed supply in the near future. Such an imbalance will serve to slow the rate of price increase during this period. For the 1980 to 1990 forecast period, aluminum supply and demand are predicted to be in an equilibrium position, with production capacity always slightly in excess of demand. This situation should have little impact on the rate of aluminum price increase during the forecast period.

TABLE II-10

ALUMINUM PRICES, 1969 - 1980

(cents per kilogram)

	U.S.* (current)	Canada** (current)	Canada (1971$)*
1969	59.92	64.52	68.56
1970	63.32	66.11	68.01
1971	63.93	64.56	64.56
1972	58.31	57.76	55.11
1973	55.84	55.90	49.60
1974	75.09	73.44	58.75
1975	87.72	89.24	64.43
1976	98.08	96.72	64.96
1977	113.06	120.35	74.84
1978	120.02	136.85	78.11
1979	131.26	153.77	80.42
1980	153.22	179.07	85.03

*   Monthly average prices for 99.5 percent pure aluminum ingots as noted in American Metal Market and converted to ¢/kg.

**   Canadian price equivalent calculated using exchange rates summarized in Table 65 of the Bank of Canada Review, December 1980.

*** Adjusted to 1971 dollar equivalents using the Consumer Price Index.

The primary reason why aluminum prices have risen and will continue to rise is the impact of increasing energy costs on production costs. During the 1970's, those smelters that relied on electric power supplied by thermal plants were seriously affected by increases in fossil fuel price increases (Japanese smelters were hardest hit with the result that some production capacity was actually taken out of service). Some smelters in other countries were forced to face higher energy costs when their contracts to purchase low-cost power from hydroelectric facilities expired. In both circumstances, producers increased their aluminum ingot prices to cover production costs while trying to remain price competitive with those smelters largely unaffected by energy cost increases. The net result was that ingot prices steadily rose during the 1970's, with some smelter locations having considerable cost advantages over others.

The impact of higher energy price can be seen in Figure II-3 which shows how the price of aluminum varied between 1969 and 1980 in real dollar terms. Prior to 1975 aluminum prices were relatively consistent in real terms, although a short term decline in real values occurred because of fluctuating exchange rates. After 1975, however, the real value of aluminum has risen by about 5.7 percent per year to reach current levels. Most of this increase is attributable to higher world energy costs, although the world supply/demand balance during this period (as noted above) had some impact.

Energy costs are predicted to have an equally important impact on aluminum costs in the 1980's. In a 1978 study of the U.S. aluminum industry, it was estimated that power from the Bonneville Power Authority, which services more than 30 percent of U.S. smelter capacity, would increase by 7.5 percent annually through to 1990 and these costs to the U.S. aluminum industry would result in real price increases of 2.5 percent annually.[24] A more recent study assumed that a three percent real rate of increase in U.S. aluminum prices was likely; this rate was based on the idea that the price of aluminum would reach $2.21 per kg. (in current U.S. dollars) by 1985, and that the rate of inflation would average seven percent per year during this period.[25] Both these rates are below the rate of real increase in aluminum prices observed during the period from 1975 to 1980.

FIGURE II-3

ALUMINUM PRICES   1969 - 1980

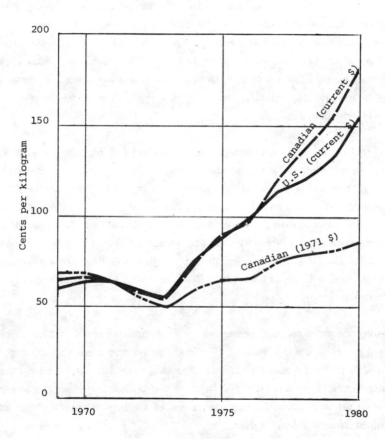

For the purposes of this forecast, two different estimates of the rate of increase in real aluminum prices will be used. The first estimate assumes an annual rate of increase in real value of two percent per year, which would see the price of aluminum hit $2.18 per kilogram (in 1980$ Cdn.) by 1990. Under these circumstances, those smelters facing energy cost increases of greater than two percent per year would become increasingly uneconomical to operate and more of the world demand would have to be met by new smelters with low cost power sources. Such a scenario would see greater shifting of smelter capacity away from Japan, Europe and the U.S. The second estimate of aluminum price increases assumes an annual four percent increase in real terms with the result that the price of aluminum would reach $2.65 (in 1980$, Cdn.) by 1990. These higher prices would allow smelters with higher than average operating costs to continue to operate economically, and fewer new smelters would be necessary to meet world aluminum demand.

Rates of real increase in aluminum prices of two and four percent per year are consistent with the other forecasts cited above. This range has been chosen to present high and low price increases and to assist in determining how sensitive the economics of a Yukon aluminum smelter would be to different price forecasts. The rates chosen are lower than the rate of real increase in aluminum price observed during the late 1970's because an overall aluminum supply/demand balance is assumed for the forecast period. Figure II-4 shows how aluminum prices would rise, in terms of both 1980$ Cdn. and 1971$ Cdn., under each of the price scenarios.

In reviewing the price forecast presented above, it must be noted that the prices quoted are prices on the U.S. market. World aluminum prices are actually higher than the U.S. prices by about $0.10/kg. The U.S. price has been used because more data on prices are available and because the United States, as the largest consumer of primary aluminum, represents one of the largest potential markets for aluminum from a Yukon smelter.

FIGURE II-4

ALUMINUM PRICE FORECAST 1980 - 1990

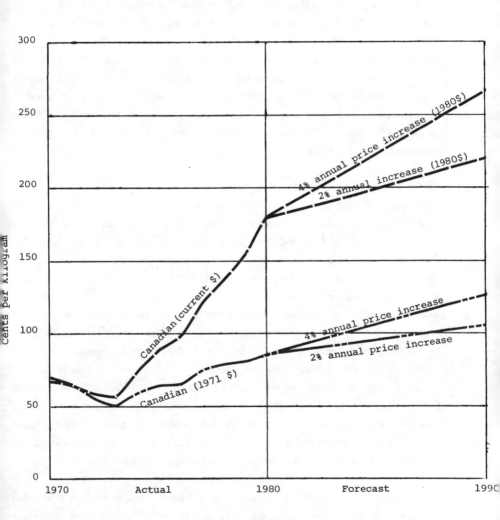

4.5   Potential Markets for a Yukon Smelter

Having established the current status of the world aluminum industry and prepared a supply/demand forecast to 1990, it is now necessary to determine how an aluminum smelter in the Yukon might fit into the overall picture. Given the aluminum supply forecast in Section 4.2, there would be no place for a Yukon smelter before 1985; production capacity under construction or in the planning stages is more than adequate to meet demand. After 1985, however, the picture is not quite so clear. Although capacity was assumed to continue to increase at about four percent per year from 1985 to 1990, this assumption was not based on any schedule of proposed smelter additions. Consequently, to meet world demand a smelter in the Yukon may be needed, but only if it can produce aluminum at lower prices than potential development sites in other countries.

The ultimate criterion for determining the economic viability of a Yukon smelter is the relationship between production costs and the price paid for the aluminum ingots produced. While this question is thoroughly dealt with in Chapter III, it is necessary to comment on the anticipated trends in aluminum prices. Based on the general agreement that the real price of aluminum will rise, forecasts of these price increases were prepared in Section 4.4. Under a scenario of a slow increase in real aluminum prices (two percent per year) the market for Yukon aluminum may be more secure because some current smelter operations would be unable to continue to profitably produce aluminum as energy prices increase. On the other hand, more rapid escalation of the real price of aluminum might be necessary to make a Yukon smelter profitable, but such increases could also result in more competition in the market for primary aluminum. Those smelters facing rising operating costs would be able to continue to produce aluminum as long as price increases offset the higher production costs. Thus, higher aluminum prices could make an aluminum smelter in the Yukon profitable to operate, but it would be more difficult to obtain a share of the market.

In reviewing the geographical location of a Yukon smelter vis-a-vis existing major aluminum markets and production capacity, three different countries must be considered as likely consumers of Yukon aluminum. Canada is the closest market for Yukon aluminum; Japan is currently having domestic aluminum supply problems; and the United States remains the largest consumer and importer of primary aluminum in the world. Each of these three potential markets is reviewed below.

(a) Canada

From a geographical perspective the Canadian market, particularly Vancouver and the Lower Mainland, is the closest potential market for Yukon aluminum. It is unlikely, however, that such a market would ever develop because most of the aluminum currently produced in Canada is exported. In 1978, for instance, Canadian exports of aluminum amounted to over 862 thousand tonnes or 82 percent of the aluminum produced that year. Most of these exports went to the United States (58 percent) and Japan (19 percent). While Canadian consumption of aluminum is likely to continue to grow throughout the 1980's, no shortages of domestically produced aluminum is ever foreseen. In addition, Alcan is currently considering new smelter capacity in Manitoba and in the vicinity of Kitimat, B.C., so that a Yukon smelter might have to face even more competition than currently exists. Considering that Alcan's Kitimat smelter is paying only about five cents per kilogram of aluminum for electricity, it is inconceivable that a Yukon smelter could never produce aluminum for less and thereby undercut Alcan aluminum to get a share of the Canadian market.[26] Thus, Canada does not present a likely market for Yukon aluminum.

(b) Japan

As noted in Section 3.3, Japan has had to make major cutbacks in its aluminum production capacity mainly because of rising energy costs. With most of its electricity generated by fossil fuel thermal plants, Japanese aluminum producers were estimated to be paying 77 cents per kilogram of aluminum for electricity in 1979. Under these conditions the government organized a cartel which reduced inventories, reduced production, scrapped some production capacity and temporarily froze other production capacity. With Japanese demand for aluminum rising throughout this period, imports of aluminum rose to 0.7 million tonnes in 1979. To further assist Japanese aluminum smelters, producers and domestic consumers negotiated an aluminum price five percent higher than the U.S. price so that operating smelters could cover their costs. As a further measure, the Japanese government has developed its own inventories.

While the measures noted above have provided short term relief for the industry, it is not likely that energy problems will improve significantly over the forecast period and many smelters may remain closed. This situation means that Japan will be increasingly reliant on imports. One estimate suggests that by 1985, Japanese aluminum demand will have risen to 2.15 million tonnes, of which 1.15 million tonnes will have to be imported.[27] This potential market appears ideally suited to take the output from a Yukon smelter and, in fact, Alcan is basing its expansion plans at Kitimat on being able to penetrate new markets in Japan.

The Japanese are also investigating ways of supplying domestic demand, with many firms having invested in the development of new smelters in other countries, particularly Australia. In reviewing the new smelters planned for Australia, Japanese investors are behind over 0.5 million tonnes per year of new capacity to be added by 1984. Japanese monies have also been invested in new smelters planned for Indonesia, Venezuela and Brazil. The net result of these investments is that Japanese smelters should continue to supply the bulk of Japanese aluminum demand, although the smelters happen to be located outside the country. Thus, Japan could prove to be a suitable market for Yukon aluminum, but the size of this potential market is much smaller than would first appear, due to the construction of new smelters outside the country. In addition, Yukon aluminum would still have to compete with aluminum from other sources, particularly from existing and new smelters at Kitimat, for a piece of the Japanese market. Thus, Japan must be considered as having a small market potential for Yukon aluminum, with the amount of aluminum likely to be purchased being dependent on the price of Yukon aluminum vis-a-vis aluminum from competing smelters.

(c) United States

Although the United States is both the largest producer and consumer of aluminum, increasing quantities are having to be imported to meet domestic demand. In 1978, for example, U.S. consumption totalled 5.1 million tonnes of which 4.3 million tonnes were produced in the United States and 0.8 million tonnes were imported (0.5 million tonnes from Canada). Prior to 1978, U.S. consumption had been growing twice as fast as domestic production, with increasing imports and more scrap recycling facilities being relied upon to fill the gap.

The main reason for production falling below consumption in the United States is that little new smelter capacity has been added since the 1975 recession. The rapidly increasing cost of power in the U.S. is thought to be the major factor inhibiting development of new smelters. In 1979 it was estimated that power costs to U.S. smelters ranged between 6 and 66 cents per kilogram of aluminum.[28] Operating problems, particularly those related to fluorine or chlorine emissions from reduction cells, have also hindered smelter development.

A second reason for requiring more imports is that some U.S. smelter operations have had to reduce their production due to energy supply problems. Water shortages in the Columbia River drainage basin led the Bonneville Power Authority to curtail power production in late 1979 and early 1980 and this resulted in the closure of ten percent of the smelting capacity of the region. The problems in this region were further aggravated when the Bonneville Power Authority increased general power rates to about 14 mils per kilowatt hour; during the peak of the water shortage, prices paid for electricity actually reached 51 mils per kilowatt hour. During these shortages aluminum producers had to find alternate energy sources (power was imported from Canada during this time) and the prices paid for this power was often in excess of 40 mils.[29] Thus, aluminum production in the Pacific Northwest dropped off during this period and further reliance was placed on imported aluminum.

The bright spot for the aluminum industry in the U.S. has been the steady increase in aluminum prices in recent years. Such price increases have meant that idle plants and capacity in Texas and Indiana could again be started in 1980. Higher prices for aluminum also buffered the impact of rising energy prices at aluminum smelters throughout the U.S., and particularly in the Pacific Northwest.

In the future, U.S. reliance on imported aluminum is expected to grow. In Section 4.1, U.S. demand for aluminum was forecast to increase by 3.5 percent per year to 1990. Based on the review of planned additions to smelter capacity (Section 4.2), U.S. production is expected to increase by only 1.4 percent per year. Under these assumptions, aluminum imports will rise from about 0.8 million tonnes in 1978, to 1.5 million tonnes by 1985 and 2.3 million tonnes by 1990. This prediction indicates a large potential market for aluminum from a Yukon smelter.

Like Japan, however, the United States is now developing more new smelter capacity in other countries. New smelters in Australia, Brazil, Venezuela and the Philippines are now under construction and were backed in whole or in part by U.S. investors. Domestic companies are also investigating further potential smelter sites at locations near new hydrolectric projects in countries in South America and Africa, or in countries with low cost thermal energy (Middle East). When suitable locations are found, smelter construction usually occurs through joint ventures with the host governments, complete with assured supplies of low cost or subsidized power. This pattern of development suggests that a Yukon smelter would ultimately be competing with these new foreign smelters for a piece of the U.S. aluminum market. And unless the Yukon smelter were in part backed by one of the large U.S. parent firms, these smelters in foreign countries would have better access to the markets because of the corporate structure of the industry.

A second response to inadequate domestic aluminum production is that existing smelter operations are experimenting with new technologies or new operating systems to reduce energy consumption and operating costs. Examples of this include ALCOA's choride-based production process and replacement of the Soderburg anode systems. While upgrading of new smelters will be expensive, this expense will be justified if the price of aluminum continues to rise quickly. Under such a scenario, domestic production may grow slightly faster than the 1.4 percent per year assumed previously. If, on the other hand, smaller increases in aluminum prices occur, additional imports of aluminum may be required because some domestic smelter closures may be imminent.

Based on the trends and assumptions detailed above, the United States is seen to have a small market potential for Yukon aluminum. Although domestic producers will continue to supply a progessively smaller proportion of U.S. aluminum demand, U.S.-backed foreign smelters will probably be the preferred source of aluminum imports. If, however, the Yukon enjoys a significant energy price advantage over other countries, the United States could probably be relied on to purchase much of the aluminum smelted in the Yukon.

(d) Summary

Of the three likely markets for aluminum, the United States is recognized to have the greatest potential, with Japan a close second. For both countries, the demands for aluminum will require the importation of increasing quantities of primary aluminum. And while major companies from each country are actively participating in overseas smelter developments to ensure adequate aluminum supplies, the U.S. market is seen to be less protected and more accessible to Yukon aluminum than the Japanese market. Canada is assumed to have no market potential for primary aluminum from the Yukon, and will in fact remain a large aluminum exporter.

No other potential markets are foreseen. In total, the U.S., Japan, and Canada accounted for 60 percent of western world consumption of aluminum in 1978. European countries accounted for another 30 percent of western world demand but they are geographically too distant to be a steady market for Yukon aluminum. Other countries that consume aluminum include Australia, New Zealand, and various countries in Africa and South America but they typically have more than adequate aluminum production capacity already and would be major competitors with a potential Yukon smelter in years to come. Thus, a Yukon smelter would have to look to the U.S. and Japan for potential markets, and its success in penetrating those markets will depend on the cost of producing aluminum in the Yukon vis-a-vis competing smelters in foreign countries.

FOOTNOTES - CHAPTER II

(1) This figure is based on information contained in a status report on the aluminum industry as published in the 1975 edition of Mineral Facts and Problems published by the U.S. Bureau of Mines.

(2) I.A. Litvak and C.J. Maule, 1977. Alcan Aluminium Limited: A Case Study, prepared for the Royal Commission on Corporate Concentration.

(3) In 1976 a strike at the four Alcan smelters in Quebec resulted in electric power supplies being cut off, and the contents of the 4000 electrolytic cells in operation were allowed to cool and harden. Alcan officials estimated that to get the system back into operation would cost $50 million.

(4) In the study of Alcan's operations prepared for the Royal Commission on Corporate Concentration, consumption of electricity in the electrolysis reaction was shown to be about 56 to 63 GJ per tonne of aluminum.

(5) This report was entitled Assessment of Geothermal Energy as a Power Source for U.S. Aluminum Plants and was prepared by W.I. Enderlin et al in 1980 for the Battelle Memorial Institute.

(6) The journal noted is the Minining Annual Review for 1980 published by the Mining Journal.

(7) See: "Aluminum: A Decade of Change", Mining Journal, February 29, 1980.

(8) Each year Mining Journal publishes an annual review of current conditions and prospects for various commodities. The figures given were contained in the 1980 Annual Review.

(9) See footnote 3.

(10) See footnote 7.

(11) See footnote 8.

(12) Figures are for 1977 and are reported in Metal Statistics 1979 and an aluminum facts sheet published annually in conjunction with the Canadian Minerals Yearbook.

(13) These forecasts are summarized in "Aluminum's Changing Horizons" in Mining Journal, November 7, 1980.

(14) Based on remarks by W. Hobbs, Vice-President, at an international aluminum congress in Madrid in 1980; commentary on his address was included in "Aluminum's Changing Horizons", Mining Journal, November 7, 1980.

(15) Based on remarks by C. Culver, Chief Executive Office of Alcan Aluminium Ltd., to the New York Society of Financial Analysts; reported in the Toronto Globe and Mail, November 18, 1980. This forecast was also presented by C. Cross of Alcan Aluminum Ltd. as presented in the Globe and Mail, January 29, 1981.

'16) This forecast is presented in Table 12 in "Aluminum" in Mineral Facts and Problems, 1975 edition, U.S. Bureau of Mines.

17) This information was noted in Energy Intensive Industries for Alaska, Volume II: Case Analysis, prepared by the Battelle Memorial Institute in 1978.

18) The results of these forecasts are summarized in Assessment of Geothermal Energy as a Power Source for U.S. Aluminum Reduction Plants, by W.I. Enderlin et al of the Battelle Memorial Institute (1980). The growth of these forecasts are summarized below:

	1980-1985	1985-1990	1990-2000
Bureau of Mines (1978) : Mineral Commodity Profiles: Aluminum			
- Total Consumption	7.1%	4.3%	4.2%
- Primary Only	7.2%	3.9%	4.1%
Bureau of Mines (1979) : Mineral Commodity Summaries			
- Apparent Metal	7.0%	---	---
Federal Preparedness Agency (1978) Long Range Aluminum Mobilization Outlook 1985-1990			
- Total Consumption	6.5%	5.6%	---

(19) Charles Rivers Associates (1977), Commodity Supply Restrictions Study, Policy Implications of Producer Counting Supply Restrictions: The World Aluminum/ Bauxite Market, as cited in: Battelle Memorial Institute (1980), Assessment of Geothermal Energy as a Power Source for Aluminum Reduction Plants.

(20) Anthony Bird Associates, UK, as noted in "Aluminum's Changing Horizons", Mining Journal, November 7, 1980.

(21) See footnote 20.

(22) See footnote 20.

(23) Noted in a presentation by W. Hobbs of Kaiser Aluminum and Chemical Corporation in 1980 as cited in "Aluminum's Changing Horizons", Mining Journal, November 7, 1980.

(24) Battelle Memorial Institute, 1978, Energy Intensiveness Industries for Alaska, Volume II: Case Analysis.

(25) Battelle Memorial Institute, 1980, Assessment of Geothermal Energy as a Power Source for U.S. Aluminum Reduction Plants.

(26) Alcan's electrical costs for its Kitimat smelter were estimated to be 2.25 cents per pound of aluminum in 1979, "Alcan Can Meet Any Competition", The Interior News, December 19, 1979.

(27) G. Ninacs, 1978, "Aluminum", published in conjunction with the Canadian Minerals Yearbook.

(28) The cost of electricity used to make aluminum in U.S. smelters was estimated to range between 2.5 and 29 cents per pound of aluminum in 1979 as per "Alcan Can Meet Any Competition", The Interior News, December 19, 1979.

(29) Power rates for BPA noted in "Repetition of Power Crisis in Northwest Not Likely", American Metal Market - Aluminum Profile, November 11, 1980.

II   ECONOMICS OF A YUKON SMELTER

The purpose of this chapter is to assess the range of electrical power costs under which a smelter in the Yukon could economically produce aluminum and market it at world prices.   By comparing all the capital and operating costs (minus electrical power) with the project income streams calculated using the price forecasts in Chapter II, it is possible to estimate the maximum power costs that a smelter could face.   These power costs can be translated into a projected rate schedule for electricity under which a smelter could successfully operate in the Yukon.   Once the cost of power from the proposed hydroelectric projects under consideration by the Northern Canada Power Commission is established, it will then be possible to determine whether or not an aluminum smelter would be economically viable in the Yukon.

In this chapter a hypothetical aluminum smelter in the Yukon is considered. Estimates of plant size, capital cost, cost of materials and labour costs are formulated.   These costs are predicted for a number of smelter utilization capacities and are compared with the projected income streams at these capacites.   Various plant financing schemes and rates of return are also considered.   The net result of these comparisons is an estimate of the maximum electricity costs under each of the various assumptions, and the corresponding electrical power rates.

Implicit in this analysis is the assumption that the smelter would not be in operation until at least 1985.   This is based on the world aluminum supply/ demand analysis in Chapter II which suggests that existing and planned smelter capacity will meet demand until 1985.   A second consideration is that smelter construction would take about four years and would require one or more years for planning and obtaining the necessary permits.

1.0   PRODUCTION PROCESS AND SMELTER SIZE

The hypothetical aluminum complex being proposed for the Yukon would consist only of an aluminum smelter and associated facilities. A bauxite refinery would not appear to be practicable in the Yukon for two reasons. First, the volume of materials to be moved and the distance involved would make the upgrading of bauxite in the Yukon a very expensive process. Secondly, bauxite-producing countries are becoming increasingly reluctant to export bauxite for upgrading elsewhere and it would be difficult to obtain the necessary bauxite for a Yukon smelter complex. Thus, a standard smelter operation using alumina imported from Australia would appear to be best suited for a Yukon location.

The aluminum smelter proposed would use a classical Hall-Heroult process for continuous electrolytic reduction of alumina in a cryolite bath, as described in Section 1.2 of Chapter II. To maximize energy efficiency, a prebaked anode system would be utilized. The use of a prebaked anode system necessitates more capital expense but it could have potentially fewer air pollution problems due to lower fluoride emissions. To further improve energy efficiency, the design and operations modifications developed by the Sumitomo Chemical Company would be included in plant design. This means that the consumption of electrical energy would amount to 48 GJ per tonne of aluminum, a 25 percent improvement over average electrical consumption in current smelters. The smelter would produce aluminum ingot and slab suitable for import to U.S. and/or Japanese markets.

The optimum size of an aluminum smelter was estimated in 1975 to be 100,000 tonnes per year, or a multiple thereof.[1] Most new smelter complexes being planned or under construction are larger than this. Alcan's new Grand Baie smelter is eventually to be 171,000 tonnes per year, and would have three potlines of 57,000 tonnes per year capacity. Alcan's preliminary expansion plans for the Kitimat area call for three new smelters of 170,000 tonnes each. Kaiser investigated the potential for a 160,000 tonne per year smelter in southern tidewater Alaska, and Alumax has proposed a 170,000 tonne smelter in Oregon.[2] Based on this review, a similar sized smelter would seem appropriate for the Yukon.

In this analysis, smelter capacity is not a key determinant of economic feasibility because costs are calculated per tonne of aluminum output. Smelter capacity does, however, play a significant role in determining the project's impacts on the regional workforce and infrastructure and the total amount of electricity it would consume. The 170,000 tonne smelter under consideration here would require a hydroelectric generating facility of 320 MW capacity. Such a hydro development may not be compatible with the Yukon's available water resources and a smaller smelter might be more appropriate. Of course, a smaller smelter would lose some of the economies of scale experienced by a plant of 170,000 tonnes and production costs would be higher. This would mean that in order to be economically viable, a smaller smelter would have to be able to purchase electricity at even lower costs than the 170,000 tonne smelter described here. An investigation of the relationship between smelter size and the maximum cost of electricity is contained in Appendix B. At such time as the size of the Yukon hydroelectric development and the costs of power are established, the appropriate smelter size could be selected based on the information in Appendix B.

2.0 DESCRIPTION OF PLANT AND CAPITAL COSTS

The smelter complex would require an area of about 155 hectares and would house the following components:

- raw material storage facilities (primarily for alumina);

- two pot lines of 85,000 tons per year capacity;

- anode and cathode manufacturing plant;

- high voltage switch yard and rectifer station;

- warehouse and maintenance shops;

- office building and laboratories; and,

- off-gas treatment facilities.

Additional capital expenditures would be required to improve the existing transportation facilities to handle the movement of raw materials. Given the volume of materials to be moved in and out of the smelter site, the White Pass and Yukon Route has estimated that upgrading of the marine terminal at Skagway would be necessary to provide storage and unloading facilities for alumina.[3] New trackage would be required to connect the smelter site with existing rail lines, and more locomotive power would be required for hauling alumina up from Skagway to the Yukon. No other upgrading of facilities is required if the ore cars currently being used to haul ore concentrates from the Yukon could also be used to handle alumina. Capital expenditures for transportation facilities can be undertaken in either of two ways. First, the smelter company could purchase the necessary equipment as an initial capital cost associated with smelter development. Second, the White Pass and Yukon Route could purchase the equipment once a transportation agreement with the smelter company has been signed; the cost of the additional equipment would then be added into the freight rates charged for hauling ingot and raw materials. For ease of calculation, any changes in the transportation network are assumed to be undertaken as a capital expenditure by the smelter company.

Several estimates of the capital cost of alumina smelters are available. These estimates are based on the cost of smelters recently built or the anticipated cost of smelters currently under construction, and are usually noted in U.S. dollars for a variety of different years. In 1980 Canadian dollar equivalents, the estimated capital cost of aluminum smelters per tonne of aluminum produced ranged as follows:

Source	Location	Cost/Tonne Output
OECD	World	$3252[5]
Kaiser	Alaska	$3183[5]
Alcan	Grand Baie, Quebec	$2925[6]
Battelle Institute	World	$2916[7]
U.S. Bureau of Mines	World	$2628[8]
P.U.H.	Quebec	$2500[9]

The most recent of these estimates suggest that the average capital cost of new smelter capacity is approximately $2900 per tonne, excluding costs for transportation infrastructure. It should be added that as the Kaiser estimate included the cost of a marine terminal and loading facilities, the cost of a smelter in the Yukon would probably be more like $3100 per tonne in 1980 dollars.

On the basis of a smelter having an annual capacity of 170,000 tonnes per year, the total capital cost of the smelter and associated transportation facilities is estimated to be about $527 million.

In order to calculate the annual cost of running an aluminum smelter, it is necessary to determine what annual payments would be required to recover this capital investment. The method used in this analysis involves the use of a capital recovery factor, defined as the proportion of the original cost that must be paid each year to recover the capital investment, pay federal taxes and provide a reasonable rate of return on the investment. Annual capital recovery factors can vary anywhere between 10 and 30 percent of the capital investment, depending on the method of financing (debt/equity), tax rates, capital cost allowances and return on equity.

For a Yukon aluminum smelter a number of different capital recovery factors have been calculated using a variety of assumptions about financing and rate of return. Three different financing scenarios were considered: 100 percent funded from equity, 50 percent from equity/50 percent from debt, and 30 percent equity/70 percent debt.   Two different methods for calculating capital cost allowances were utilized.   The first method assumed that the capital cost allowance would average 20 percent of the eligible capital investment, computed on a declining balance commencing the first year of operation; the second method assumed a capital cost allowance of 10 percent of the eligible capital investment. The federal tax rate of 43 percent for manufacturing and processing industries was assumed to apply to a Yukon smelter. Rates of return on equity of 15 and 20 percent were used to ensure a normal and high return on investments. A summary of these and other assumptions used to calculate the appropriate capital recovery factors is included as Appendix A. As a base case, however, it was assumed that the smelter would be entirely financed from equity, have a capital cost allowance of 20 percent and yield a 15 percent return on investment. Under these conditions, a capital recovery factor of 19.7 percent was calculated; this suggests an annualized cost of $103.8 million (1980$) for the aluminum smelter. Under various other financing and accounting assumptions, capital recovery factors of between 12.7 and 31.8 percent were calculated. These factors suggest that the annualized capital cost of the smelter complex might range between $66.9 million and $167.6 million. The impact of these alternate methods of financing on the economics of a Yukon aluminum smelter is discussed in Section 7.0.

3.0 MATERIAL REQUIREMENTS AND COSTS

The quantities of raw materials required to produce one tonne of primary aluminum were previously identified in Section 2.3 of Chapter II and summarized in Figure II-2. For a smelter having a capacity of 170,000 tons per year the material requirements would be as follows:

Material	Per Tonne Aluminum	Annual Plant Requirements
Alumina	1.9 tonnes	323,000 tonnes
Cryolite	35 kg.	5,950 tonnes
Aluminum Fluoride	20 kg.	3,400 tonnes
Fluorspar	2 kg.	350 tonnes
Petroleum Coke	520 kg.	88,400 tonnes
Pitch	150 kg.	25,500 tonnes
TOTAL	2.627 tonnes	446,590 tonnes

Estimates of material costs are very difficult to obtain because many smelters purchase raw materials from subsidiary or affiliated companies at non-market prices. However, a number of previous smelter studies have estimated raw materials costs and these estimates form the basis for this analysis.

3.1 Alumina

Alumina is, of course, the most important raw material used in the smelting process, and great quantities are consumed. Australia, as noted earlier, is the most accessible alumina producing country and would no doubt be the source of supply for a Yukon smelter. The price of alumina from Australia has risen sharply in recent years, from about $59 (U.S.) per tonne in 1971 to about $147 (U.S.) per tonne in 1979. Despite this increase, a recent study by Resources for the Future shows that Australian alumina entering the United States is priced well below alumina produced in the United States and other countries.[10] For 1980, the price of Australian alumina is estimated to be $180 per tonne in Candian dollars.

Alumina prices are expected to continue rising in real terms throughout the forecast period. Between 1980 and 1990 the price of alumina has been estimated by the Battelle Memorial Institute to increase by 1.2 percent pear year,[11] a rate well below the 3.3 percent annual real growth observed between 1971 and 1979. For the purposes of this forecast, the real price of alumina is forecast to rise by two percent per year throughout the forecast period. This assumption would mean that the price of alumina would reach $200 (Cdn.) per tonne by 1985 and $220 by 1990; this price does not include the cost of transportation from Australia.

3.2 Bath Materials

The materials used in the electrolyte bath include cryolite, aluminum fluoride and fluorspar. In 1978 the cost of these materials was estimated to be about $550 (U.S.) per tonne (including freight and insurance costs).[12] Cryolite is the most expensive of the bath ingredients and was estimated to cost about $570 (U.S.) per tonne in 1975.[13] The cost of aluminum fluoride, by comparison, was only about $390 per tonne at that time.[14] No prices for fluorspar were available.

For this analysis, the cost of bath materials is estimated to be $750 per tonne in 1980 Canadian dollars. This estimate assumes that there has been no real increase in the price of these materials since 1978. Real prices increases in the future are also not expected, according to assumptions by the Battelle Memorial Institute.[15] This assumption has been adopted in this forecast.

3.3 Anode and Cathode Materials

Petroleum coke, pitch and some anthracite coal are required to manufacture the prebaked anodes and to line the pots. In a 1980 study the cost of these materials was estimated to be about $90 (U.S.) per tonne in 1976 dollars;[16] a second study in 1978 estimated the cost of carbon and pitch to be about $115 (U.S.) per tonne (including freight and insurance).[17] These figures are relatively compatible, given that transportation and insurance costs are about $10 per tonne, and that the rate of inflation was about eight percent during the time period. The 1980 price equivalent in Canadian dollars for petroleum coke and pitch is estimated to be $155 per tonne.

As potential forms of energy, it is predicted that the real price of pitch and petroleum coke will rise during the forecast period. In their most recent forecast, the Battelle Memorial Institute estimated the annual rate of increase in real price to be about 4.7 percent for the study period.[18] Such rates probably reflect U.S. expectations about future world oil prices. As Canadian oil prices are kept below world prices, a rate of 4.7 percent per year is thought to be inappropriate for a Canadian smelter operation. For this forecast the real price of the anode and cathode materials is estimated to increase at a rate of 2.5 percent per year.

3.4 Total Material Costs

Based on the quantities of materials and the cost information presented above, the cost of the raw materials required to operate the proposed smelter would amount to about $83 million in 1980. As the real costs of some materials are expected to increase, the cost of raw materials would rise to about $92 million (1980$) by 1985 and to over $100 million by 1990. These costs are broken down by materials as follows:

	(millions of 1980 dollars)		
	1980	1985	1990
Alumina	$58.1	$64.6	$ 71.1
Bath Materials	7.3	7.3	7.3
Anode & Cathode Materials	17.7	19.9	22.8
TOTAL	$83.1	$91.8	$101.2

4.0 WORKFORCE

Construction of an aluminum smelter in the Yukon would generate both long and short term employment opportunities. During the four year construction period, total construction employment is estimated at 2000 man-years.[19] This construction period is slightly longer than for smelters in other locations but considerations of climate and lack of infrastructure in the Yukon suggest that a longer construction period is warranted. During the peak years of construction (in the third year), a maximum workforce of 1400 is estimated [20]; this compares to an existing total workforce in the Yukon of about 9,700 people.[21] The construction payroll is estimated to be about $58 million (1980$), assuming that other regional demands for construction labour do not escalate labour rates.[22] These labour costs represent about 11 percent of the capital cost of the project.

Estimates of the workforce required to operate a smelter of 170,000 tonnes per year capacity range between 800 and 1200 persons.[23] The latter estimate is probably the more appropriate given that operation of the marine terminal will require additional labour and that climate and other Yukon working conditions may necessitate additional manpower. A manning roster for the aluminum smelter is expected to resemble the following:[24]

Operators, craftsmen, clerks and technicians	1090
Foremen, junior professionals	70
General foreman, supervisor	15
Professionals	15
Management	10
TOTAL	1200

Current average wages in the primary metal industries in British Columbia are about $23,000, based on recent Statistics Canada information.[25] And, as wage scales for unionized labour in the Yukon are similar to wages for corresponding unions in British Columbia, the average annual wage for labour in the proposed smelter would also be $23,000 in 1980. Thus, the total wages and salaries paid to smelter employees would be $27.6 million (1980$) or $160 per tonne of aluminum produced. No increases in the real costs of labour is expected for the forecast period.

In reviewing the labour force estimates, it must be mentioned that the size and available skills of the present workforce in the Yukon would be unable to meet either the long or short term labour demands of an aluminum smelter. Actual construction and operation of a Yukon smelter would require importation of a considerable labour force and associated infrastructure. Introduction of such a large labour force would create major social and economic impacts on communities in the Yukon and various types of costs and benefits would result. While these economic and social costs should be included in an overall evaluation of the desirability of a Yukon smelter, they are beyond the scope of this analysis and have not been considered in detail.

5.0   OTHER COSTS

In operating a smelter a variety of other costs must be incurred, including charges for energy, taxes, and transportation. These costs for an aluminum smelter in the Yukon are estimated below.

5.1   Transportation

With the Yukon being landlocked and the proposed smelter being located near Whitehorse, transportation of alumina and finished aluminum ingot is a major consideration. The most direct method of transportation would entail routing the materials through the port of Skagway, Alaska, and then shipping them by rail to Whitehorse. Based on discussions with the White Pass and Yukon Route, such movement of goods would be welcomed although certain capital expenditures would be necessary to handle the volumes of materials required. Such expenditures would include alumina storage facilities and loading-unloading facilities at Skagway, more locomotives and new trackage to the smelter; the cost of these facilities is assumed to be part of the overall capital cost of the project. Estimation of the cost per tonne per kilometre to move materials between Skagway and Whitehorse is a very difficult process as there are numerous factors to be considered. However, the White Pass and Yukon Route has guessed that they would charge about $22 per tonne to move the necessary materials, as long as they faced no major capital expenditures.[26] Assuming that all raw materials for the smelter are imported to the Yukon, over 616,000 tonnes of materials would be shipped to and from the smelter each year, at a cost of $13.6 million. A second transportation cost not discussed previously is that of moving some materials - specifically, alumina - from their source to Skagway. Recent information presented by Resources for the Future suggests that in 1979, the cost of transporting and insuring a cargo of alumina from Australia to U.S. ports averaged $8.80 (U.S.) per ton.[27] The equivalent cost in 1980 Canadian dollars would be about $12 per tonne. This would add another $3.9 million to the overall cost of transporting goods to and from a Yukon smelter. The average cost of transporting these materials per tonne of aluminum produced would be about $103, given the assumptions noted above.

5.2 Energy Costs

The cost of energy required for an aluminum smelter is the largest operating expense. Electrical requirements amount to 48 GJ per tonne of aluminum produced, or a total of 8.16 PJ for a smelter of 170,000 tonnes per year. Similarly, natural gas or oil is required for anode/cathode preparation and other uses; the amount of fossil fuel required amounts to about 13 GJ per tonne of aluminum or a total of 2.2 PJ for the smelter. As the cost of electricity to be provided by a new hydroelectric project is unknown at this point of the analysis, electric power costs for a smelter are considered elsewhere. The cost of fossil fuel energy is estimated in this section.

Although the Yukon is not currently serviced by either an oil or natural gas pipeline, the development of the Foothills pipeline will provide a reliable source of natural gas for industrial development in the Yukon. This pipeline is expected to be in operation in 1985.

The price of the required natural gas is quite speculative at this time and will depend on who is actually selling natural gas to the smelter operation. The source of the natural gas would be Alaska, and the smelter would have the option of purchasing natural gas directly from Alaska at a price based on the cost of producing the gas plus a pipeline tariff. However, given that Canadian prices for natural gas would be below the price for Alaskan gas, a Yukon smelter might choose to purchase gas at Alberta prices through a gas-swap arrangement with Foothills. The rationale for choosing the latter method for purchasing natural gas is shown by the following price forecasts:

	1985	1986	1987	1988	1989	1980
Alberta/Saskatchewan[28]						
border price $1980 $/GJ	2.35	2.58	2.88	3.12	3.29	3.42
current $/GJ	3.14	3.57	4.08	4.55	4.97	5.37
Alaskan gas						
estimated price - current $/GJ	4.65	4.81	4.99	5.15	5.29	5.46

This comparison clearly shows that natural gas purchased from Alaska would be more expensive throughout the forecast period. For this reason the calculation of the cost of natural gas used in a Yukon smelter is based on the Alberta/Saskatchewan border price forecast (above) plus $0.30 per GJ as a distribution cost. With these assumptions the natural gas required by the smelter would cost $4.4 million in 1980 and rise to $5.8 million (1980$) by 1985 and $8.2 million (1980$) by 1990. On a cost per tonne of aluminum basis, natural gas costs are estimated to be $26 in 1980, $34 in 1985 and $48 by 1990.

5.3 Other Costs

A number of other operating costs must also be included in the analysis. Such costs include payments for plant maintenance materials, office overheads and other materials used in the smelter. Payments for the operation of pollution control devices and insurance are also included in this category. The actual costs of such expenditures are difficult to determine. Estimates of between $90 and $110 (1978 U.S.$) per tonne of aluminum are noted in two different studies.[30] Based on the more severe operating conditions faced by a Yukon smelter, it is estimated that these other operating costs will be at the upper end of the range indicated. After inflating this figure to 1980 Canadian dollar terms, an estimate of $150 per tonne of aluminum is assumed for this cost component. During a year of operating the smelter at capacity, these other operating costs would amount to $25.5 million (1980$). No increase in the real cost of these materials is foreseen for the study period.

5.4 Local Taxes

One last form of operating expenses is that of local taxes. Depending on smelter location, these taxes would be payable either to the Yukon Territory or the City of Whitehorse. In both cases, the tax assessment is based on the market value of the land plus the replacement value of the smelter buildings and equipment.[31] Within the City of Whitehorse, the tax payable is based on 1.2 percent of the assessed value; this would mean local taxes of $6.3 million (1980$) on the estimated capital cost of the smelter ($527 million). Outside Whitehorse the territorial tax rate of one percent of assessed value is payable; this amounts to about $5.3 million (1980$) per year.

6.0 SUMMARY OF SMELTER COSTS AND REVENUES

In summarizing smelter costs and revenues, it is necessary to specify what utilization of production capacity the smelter can be expected to operate at. Historically, many smelters have reported operating at or above 100 percent capacity under certain conditions. The long term outlook for the industry in general suggests, however, that as production capacity will exceed aluminum demand (see Section 4.3 in Chapter II), most smelters would be operating at about 90 percent capacity. In the event that aluminum demands increase more slowly than expected, a capacity utilization rate of 80 percent has also been considered. These capacity utilization factors would affect both the income and operating costs of the plant but would have little impact on the annualized capital cost of the smelter.

6.1 Smelter Income

Table III-1 summarizes the estimated income of a Yukon smelter under the three operating regimes noted above. A second factor crucial to calculation of the income stream is the rate at which aluminum prices are expected to increase in real terms throughout the forecast period. If aluminum prices increase by two percent per year, smelter revenues would be about $303 million in 1985 and would rise to $334 million by 1990. Smelter revenues would increase from $334 million to $406 million over the same period if aluminum prices increase by four percent per year. This estimate assumes operation at 90 percent of capacity.

6.2 Operating Costs

Smelter operating costs include raw material costs, wages and salaries, transportation costs, natural gas costs, Yukon taxes and other operating costs. Each of these costs has been calculated separately for the Yukon smelter in preceding sections of this chapter. A summary of these costs for the period 1985 to 1990 is presented in Table III-2. Total operating costs range from $172 million in 1985 to $183 million in 1990, assuming a capacity utilization factor of 100 percent. Total operating costs for a smelter operating at 80 or 90 percent of capacity are summarized for the forecast period in Table III-3. In reviewing these costs it must be noted that the cost of electricity has been purposely omitted. Depending on the unit cost of electricity, the cost of electricity could prove to be a significant addition to total operating costs.

6.3 Annualized Capital Costs

As described in Section 2.0, the annualized capital cost of an aluminum smelter in the Yukon would depend on how the project is financed, the method of calculating capital cost allowance, and the rate of return on investment. The assumptions outlined in Section 2.0, the resulting capital recovery factor, and the estimates of annualized capital cost are summarized in Table III-4. Although the annualized capital cost estimates range from $66.9 million to $167.6 million, the estimate of $103.8 is thought to be the most appropriate case because of the assumptions used in calculating the capital recovery factor. This estimate is considered as the base case for the calculation of electrical costs of aluminum production in Section 7.0. A sensitivity analysis on the other assumptions is also undertaken in Section 7.0.

TABLE III-1

FORECAST OF ALUMINUM SMELTER REVENUES

(millions of 1980$)

	Two Percent Increase in Aluminum Prices			Four Percent Increase in Aluminum Prices		
	100% Capacity	90% Capacity	80% Capacity	100% Capacity	90% Capacity	80% Capacity
1985	336.3	302.7	269.0	370.6	333.5	296.5
1986	343.4	309.1	274.7	384.2	345.8	307.4
1987	350.2	315.2	280.2	401.2	361.1	321.0
1988	357.0	321.3	285.6	416.5	374.9	333.2
1989	363.8	327.4	291.0	433.5	390.2	346.8
1990	370.6	333.5	296.5	450.5	405.5	360.4

TABLE III-2

SUMMARY OF ALUMINUM SMELTER OPERATING COSTS

(millions of 1980$)

	1985	1986	1987	1988	1989	1990
Raw materials	91.8	93.6	95.5	97.3	99.2	101.2
Labour	27.6	27.6	27.6	27.6	27.6	27.6
Transportation	17.5	17.5	17.5	17.5	17.5	17.5
Natural Gas	5.8	6.4	7.0	7.6	7.9	8.2
Other Operating Costs	25.5	25.5	25.5	25.5	25.5	25.5
Yukon Taxes	5.3	5.3	5.3	5.3	5.3	5.3
Total	173.5	175.9	178.4	180.8	183.0	185.3

TABLE III-3

FORECAST OF ALUMINUM SMELTER OPERATING COSTS

(millions of 1980$)

	100 Percent Capacity Utilization	90 Percent Capacity Utilization	80 Percent Capacity Utilization
1985	173.5	156.2	138.8
1986	175.9	158.3	140.7
1987	178.4	160.6	142.7
1988	180.8	162.7	144.6
1989	183.0	164.7	146.4
1990	185.3	166.8	148.2

TABLE III-4

ESTIMATED ANNUALIZED CAPITAL COSTS OF A YUKON ALUMINUM SMELTER

Financing (Equity)	Capital Cost Allowance	Return on Equity	Capital Recovery Factor	Annualized Capital Cost ($ million)
100%	20%	15%	19.7%	103.8
100%	20%	20%	30.0%	158.1
100%	10%	15%	21.0%	110.7
100%	10%	20%	31.8%	167.6
50%	20%	15%	14.7%	77.5
50%	20%	20%	20.6%	108.6
30%	20%	15%	12.7%	66.9
30%	20%	20%	16.8%	88.5

7.0   ESTIMATION OF ELECTRIC POWER COSTS

By subtracting plant operating costs and the annualized capital cost from smelter revenues, it is possible to determine the maximum amount that the smelter could pay for electric power and still remain economically viable. These calculations have been done for a number of different smelter operating regimes and the results are summarized in Tables III-5 to III-10 and compared in Figure III-1.

As a base case estimate, it is assumed that the smelter will operate at 90 percent capacity and that the price of primary aluminum will rise by two percent per year. The smelter is assumed to be financed 100 percent from equity and is expected to pay a 15 percent rate of return after tax; these assumptions correspond to Table III-6. Given these assumptions, it appears that electrical power costs of between 22 and 32 mills over the period 1985 to 1990 would make an aluminum smelter in the Yukon a viable operation. This suggests an electrical cost of between 29 and 42 cents per kilogram of aluminum produced.

In comparison, recent figures have suggested that Alcan currently pays between 33 and 64 cents for the electricity necessary to produce one kilogram of aluminum.[32] Other smelters face even higher electrical energy costs, ranging from 50 to 70 cents per kilogram of aluminum. Thus, in order to be competitive in the world aluminum market, a Yukon smelter would have to be able to purchase electricity at a rate close to the price that Alcan is presently paying.

If world demand for aluminum increases more slowly than expected, and utilization of capacity is reduced to 80 percent, power costs would have to be lower than the base case for the smelter to remain competitive. Maximum electric power costs would have to be between 15 and 25 mills under these circumstances (see Table III-7). The impact of different smelter utilization rates is shown graphically in Figure III-1.

The impact of aluminum prices rising at four percent per year would be to make a Yukon smelter economically viable at even higher electrical power costs.

TABLE III-5

CALCULATION OF MAXIMUM ELECTRICITY RATES
UNDER WHICH A YUKON SMELTER COULD OPERATE

CASE A

(millions of 1980$)

	1985	1986	1987	1988	1989	1990
Revenues	336.3	343.3	350.2	357.0	363.8	370.6
Operating Cost	173.5	175.9	178.4	180.8	183.0	185.3
Capital Cost	103.8	103.8	103.8	103.8	103.8	103.8
Electricity Costs	59.0	63.7	68.0	72.4	77.0	81.5
Estimated Electricity Rates						
- $/GJ	7.20	7.77	8.29	8.83	9.39	9.94
- mills/kWh	25	27	29	31	33	35

Assumptions:

   Aluminum prices - real increase of 2 percent per year.
   Operating capacity - smelter operates at 100 percent capacity.
   Financing - debt/equity - 100 percent
   Capital Cost Allowance - 20 percent declining balance.
   Capital Recovery Factor - 15 percent.

80

TABLE III-6

CALCULATION OF MAXIMUM ELECTRICITY RATES
UNDER WHICH A YUKON SMELTER COULD OPERATE

CASE B

(millions of 1980$)

	1985	1986	1987	1988	1989	1990
Revenues	302.7	309.1	315.2	321.3	327.4	333.5
Operating Cost	156.2	158.3	160.6	162.7	164.7	166.8
Capital Cost	103.8	103.8	103.8	103.8	103.8	103.8
Electricity Costs	42.7	47.0	50.8	54.8	58.9	62.9
Estimated Electricity Rates						
- $/GJ	5.85	6.44	6.96	7.51	8.07	8.62
- mills/kWh	21	23	25	27	29	31

Assumptions:

Aluminum prices - real increase of 2 percent per year.
Operating capacity - smelter operates at 90 percent capacity.
Financing - debt/equity - 100 percent
Capital Cost Allowance - 20 percent declining balance.
Capital Recovery Factor - 15 percent.

TABLE III-7

CALCULATION OF MAXIMUM ELECTRICITY RATES
UNDER WHICH A YUKON SMELTER COULD OPERATE

CASE C

(millions of 1980$)

	1985	1986	1987	1988	1989	1990
Revenues	269.0	274.7	280.2	285.6	291.0	296.5
Operating Cost	138.3	140.7	142.7	144.6	146.4	148.2
Capital Cost	103.8	103.8	103.8	103.8	103.8	103.8
Electricity Costs	26.4	30.2	33.7	37.2	40.8	44.5
Estimated Electricity Rates						
- $/GJ	4.06	4.65	5.18	5.72	6.28	6.85
- mills/kWh	14	16	18	20	22	24

Assumptions:

    Aluminum prices - real increase of 2 percent per year.
    Operating capacity - smelter operates at 80 percent capacity.
    Financing - debt/equity - 100 percent
    Capital Cost Allowance - 20 percent declining balance.
    Capital Recovery Factor - 15 percent.

TABLE III-8

CALCULATION OF MAXIMUM ELECTRICITY RATES
UNDER WHICH A YUKON SMELTER COULD OPERATE

CASE D

(millions of 1980$)

	1985	1986	1987	1988	1989	1990
Revenues	370.6	384.2	401.2	416.2	433.5	450.5
Operating Cost	173.5	175.9	178.4	180.8	183.0	185.3
Capital Cost	103.8	103.8	103.8	103.8	103.8	103.8
Electricity Costs	93.3	104.5	119.0	131.9	146.7	161.4
Estimated Electricity Rates						
- $/GJ	11.38	12.74	14.51	16.09	17.89	19.68
- mills/kWh	40	45	52	57	64	70

Assumptions:

Aluminum prices - real increase of 4 percent per year.
Operating capacity   -   smelter operates at 100 percent capacity.
Financing - debt/equity - 100 percent
Capital Cost Allowance - 20 percent declining balance.
Capital Recovery Factor - 15 percent.

TABLE III-9

CALCULATION OF MAXIMUM ELECTRICITY RATES
UNDER WHICH A YUKON SMELTER COULD OPERATE

CASE E

(millions of 1980$)

	1985	1986	1987	1988	1989	1990
Revenues	333.5	345.8	361.1	374.9	390.2	405.5
Operating Cost	156.2	158.3	160.6	162.7	164.7	166.8
Capital Cost	103.8	103.8	103.8	103.8	103.8	103.8
Electricity Costs	73.5	83.7	96.7	108.3	121.7	134.8
Estimated Electricity Rates						
- $/GJ	10.07	11.47	13.25	14.84	16.67	18.47
- mills/kWh	36	41	47	53	60	66

Assumptions:

Aluminum prices - real increase of 4 percent per year.
Operating capacity - smelter operates at 90 percent capacity.
Financing - debt/equity - 100 percent
Capital Cost Allowance - 20 percent declining balance.
Capital Recovery Factor - 15 percent.

TABLE III-10

CALCULATION OF MAXIMUM ELECTRICITY RATES
UNDER WHICH A YUKON SMELTER COULD OPERATE

CASE F

(millions of 1980$)

	1985	1986	1987	1988	1989	1990
Revenues	296.5	307.4	321.0	333.2	346.8	360.4
Operating Cost	138.8	140.7	142.7	144.6	146.4	148.2
Capital Cost	103.8	103.8	103.8	103.8	103.8	103.8
Electricity Costs	53.9	62.9	74.5	84.8	96.6	108.4
Estimated Electricity Rates						
- $/GJ	8.29	9.68	11.46	13.05	14.86	16.68
- mills/kWh	29	34	41	46	53	60

Assumptions:

Aluminum prices - real increase of 4 percent per year.
Operating capacity - smelter operates at 80 percent capacity.
Financing - debt/equity - 100 percent
Capital Cost Allowance - 20 percent declining balance.
Capital Recovery Factor - 15 percent.

FIGURE III-1

MAXIMUM ELECTRICITY RATES
UNDER WHICH A YUKON SMELTER COULD OPERATE

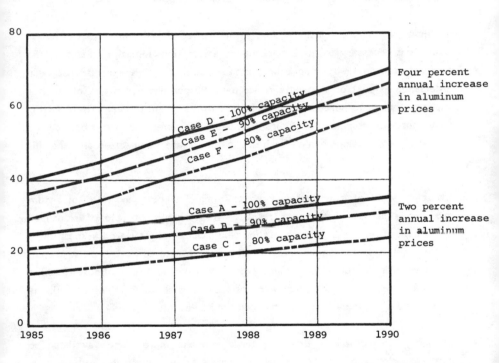

Depending on the degree of smelter utilization, electrical costs could range between 31 and 42 mills in 1985, increasing to between 61 and 72 mills in 1990, and the smelter would remain economically viable. It must be remembered, however, that such high prices for aluminum would benefit smelters throughout the world and increase competition amongst aluminum producers for available markets. Under such conditions a Yukon smelter with power costs of 30 to 40 mills would definitely enjoy an advantage over many other smelters.

To further assess the relationship between smelter viability and electric power costs, it is necessary to alter some of the assumptions regarding financing and rate of return while holding other factors constant. This exercise has been undertaken as part of Appendix A assuming 90 percent utilization of smelter capacity and a two percent annual increase in aluminum prices. The resulting power costs are compared in Figure III-2, based on Tables A-2 to A-9 in Appendix A, and the assumptions behind each cost estimate are summarized on Table III-11.

Changing some of the assumptions regarding financing and rate of return produces some very interesting results. If a 20 percent rate of return on investment is required, power costs must be substantially lowered in most cases if the smelter is to remain viable. This higher rate of return on a project financed entirely from equity would prohibit development until almost 1990 and the would require maximum power costs of from 1 to 5 mills, an unlikely occurrence when a new hydroelectric plant must be built.

Changing the method of financing tends to make more money available to purchase electricity. Consequently, power rates available to purchase electricity could be significantly higher. Under 30 percent equity financing, power costs could be as high as 29 to 40 mills in 1985, and a Yukon smelter could produce aluminum for sale at world prices and still produce a 15 to 20 percent return on investment. Financing using 50 percent equity would mean that Yukon electric power rates in 1985 could range between 19 and 35 mills (depending on the expected rate of return) and the smelter would be competitive on world markets.

FIGURE III-2

IMPACT OF ALTERNATE METHODS OF FINANCING AND
RATES OF RETURN ON MAXIMUM ELECTRICITY RATES
UNDER WHICH A YUKON ALUMINUM SMELTER COULD OPERATE*

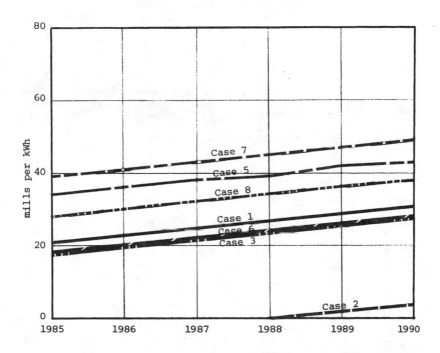

*   For a description of the assumptions underlying these price forecasts
see Table III-11 (next page) and Appendix A. Case 4 would not appear
on the Figure until after 1990.

TABLE III-11

ASSUMPTIONS BEHIND CALCULATIONS
OF MAXIMUM ELECTRICITY RATES IN FIGURE III-2

	Method of Financing (% equity)	Capital Cost Allowance (%)	Rate of Return (%)
Case 1	100	20	15
Case 2	100	20	20
Case 3	100	10	15
Case 4	100	10	20
Case 5	50	20	15
Case 6	50	20	20
Case 7	30	20	15
Case 8	30	20	20

Changing the method for calculating the capital cost allowance has a small impact on maximum power rates. By decreasing the proportion of the eligible capital investment included in the capital cost allowance calculation from 20 percent to ten percent, the cost of electricity must be lowered by from three to four mills for the aluminum smelter to remain economic.

FOOTNOTES - CHAPTER III

(1) Litvak, I.A. and C.J. Maule, 1977. Alcan Aluminium Limited: A Case Study, Royal Commission on Corporate Concentration.

(2) These examples were cited in a study of the potential for an aluminum smelter in Alaska entitled Energy Intensive Industries For Alaska Volume II: Case Analysis and prepared by the Battelle Memorial Institute in 1978. In the case study a hypothetical smelter of 180,000 short tons per year (163,000 tonnes per year) was considered.

(3) Based on discussions with the Senior Manager, Vancouver, White Pass and Yukon Route.

(4) OECD, 1977. Pollution Control Costs in the Primary Aluminium Industry, Paris.

(5) See footnote 2.

(6) Noted in "Alcan project and Pechiney study point to growth of Quebec aluminum industry", The Globe and Mail, December 16, 1980.

(7) Battelle Memorial Institute, 1980. Assessment of Geothermal Energy as a Power Source for U.S. Aluminum Reduction Plants.

(8) U.S. Bureau of Mines, 1975. Mineral Facts and Problems, Bulletin 667, U.S. Dept. of the Interior.

(9) See footnote 6.

(10) Resources for the Future, 1980. World Mineral Trends and U.S. Supply Problems.

(11) See footnote 7.

(12) See footnote 2.

(13) See footnote 7 and footnote 4.

(15) See footnote 7.

(16) See footnote 7.

(17) See footnote 2.

(18) See footnote 7.

(19) See footnote 2.

(20) See footnote 2.

(21) Estimate provided by Yukon Chamber of Commerce.

(22) This assumes an average annual income of $29,000 for the construction workforce and reflects an average weekly wage of about $550 for construction workers in B.C. in 1980 (Statistics Canada, Catalogue 72-202).

(23) See footnote 2.

(24) See footnote 2.

(25) Statistics Canada, Catalogue 72-002, Employment Earnings and Hours.

(26) See footnote 3.

(27) See footnote 10.

(28) Based on natural gas price assumptions in:

Canadian Resourcecon Ltd., 1981. Twenty Five Year Forecast of Natural Gas Demand in Alberta 1981-2005, prepared for Alberta and Southern Gas Co. Ltd. and TransCanada Pipelines.

Estimated natural gas prices in current dollar terms assumes eight percent annual inflation.

(29) This price is the average of the Alaska/Yukon and Yukon/B.C. border prices for natural gas as calculated by Foothills Pipelines.

(30) See footnotes 2 and 7.

(31) Yukon tax information based on personal communications with Tax Assessment Office, Yukon Territorial government.

(32) These figures quoted in "Mixed outlook for aluminum producers", The Financial Post, December 27, 1980.

IV   SUMMARY

Until the cost of electric power to be provided by hydroelectric development in the Yukon is known, no conclusions regarding the feasibility of an aluminum smelter in the Yukon can be stated. The economic assessment of the conceptual 170,000 tonne smelter described in Chapter III suggests that if electric power were to cost less than 10 mills per kWh, smelter development in the next decade would be justified under most of the different operating and financing schemes considered. If power costs were to be in the order of 30 mills per kWh, a Yukon smelter would be feasible only under certain financing schemes or if the world price for aluminum were to rise at four percent per year (rather than two percent per year). At electric power costs of 40 mills per kWh, the feasibility of a Yukon smelter could be assured only if the most optimistic aluminum price forecast is adopted. At 50 mills per kWh, smelter construction would not be justified until 1990, even assuming that aluminum prices increase rapidly. Thus, depending on the eventual cost of electric power in the Yukon, an aluminum smelter might well be an economically viable industrial development for the Yukon.

Within the world aluminum market there appear to be no insurmountable obstacles to smelter development in the Yukon. Given the aluminum supply/demand forecast of Chapter II, there would be no need for a Yukon smelter until at least 1985, however, the lead time to build the smelter and the hydroelectric generating facilities is also five years. The most likely markets for Yukon aluminum would be the United States and Japan - both countries have demands far in excess of domestic supply - but to successfully penetrate these markets, a Yukon smelter will have to have lower electric energy costs than U.S. and Japanese-financed smelters currently under construction or being planned in Third World countries.

In the overall world market, a Yukon smelter would be competing most directly with planned smelters in Australia, Brazil and Venezuela. Each of these three countries has direct access to bauxite and alumina and relatively low cost power resources - Australia has coal, Brazil has hydroelectric potential and Venezuela has petroleum reserves. How a Yukon smelter will fare in competition with these new developments will ultimately depend on the relative costs of electric power in each country.

The only major problem in operating a Yukon smelter may be to find a steady source of alumina. Australia is the logical source of this alumina but they have an implicit policy to develop their domestic aluminum smelting capacity rather than export alumina for upgrading elsewhere. Such a policy might stand in the way of reaching a long term agreement with Australia to supply alumina to a Yukon smelter.

Part of this alumina supply problem might be resolved if the Yukon smelter were developed by one of the six large aluminum-producing companies having alumina-producing subsidiaries or affiliates in Australia. Other benefits of development by one of the larger producers would include purchasing raw materials at transfer prices, having better access to markets, and having management experienced in the workings of the world aluminum industry. However, such producers are typically large multinational corporations and the potential impacts of foreign investment by these companies (except, perhaps, Alcan) must be assessed before the decision is made to encourage smelter development in the Yukon.

Before concluding this summary there are two points that merit further attention. First, the economic analysis of the conceptual smelter is based on the assumption that no financial concessions are given by governments to encourage smelter development in the Yukon. Obviously tax incentives, preferential power rates and government participation in funding could significantly alter the results of the analysis in Chapter III, so that smelter construction would be justifiable with even higher electric power costs. It is difficult to anticipate just what forms of government assistance might be adopted and so no allowance for development incentives has been included in this study.

The second point to be made is that aluminum smelter development would have major impacts on the economic and social fabric of the Yukon. A workforce of 1200 persons would represent a 12 percent increase over the existing Yukon workforce, and the population of the Yukon would swell dramatically with the addition of workers and their families. Smelter expenditures on labour and supplies would also have multiplier effects on the regional economy, bringing in more people and more money. Such changes may or may not be compatible with the social and economic objectives of the Yukon and further investigations of the overall impact of smelter development on the Yukon would need to be undertaken as part of future smelter feasibility studies.

APPENDIX A

ESTIMATION OF CAPITAL RECOVERY FACTORS

APPENDIX A

ESTIMATION OF CAPITAL RECOVERY FACTORS

A.1 General

The capital recovery factors used in this analysis represent the annual revenue required solely to recover the capital investment, including a reasonable after tax rate of return on the equity component of the investment. Capital costs are estimated in constant dollars (i.e. excluding inflation).

Annual capital recovery factors can vary anywhere between 10 and 30 percent of the capital investment depending on the method of financing (debt/equity), tax rates, capital cost allowances and return on equity. No single CRF is right for all conditions; rather, a set of conditions can be specified and the appropriate CRF determined for those conditions. Any changes in conditions gives rise to a different CRF. This appendix sets out the base conditions used to determine CRFs.

A.2 Capital Investment

Where possible, capital cost estimates have been adjusted to include the costs of land and equipment, working capital and start up.

Interest during construction is not included in the capital investments; however, the capital recovery factors include allowances for this cost where applicable.

Design and construction of the type and scale of aluminum smelter under consideration would take about four years. The capital investment, in constant dollars, is assumed to be spent as follows: 10 percent in year 1, 20 percent in year 2, 50 percent in year 3 and 20 percent in year 4.

A.3 Source of Funds

For the baseline analysis the total capital investment is assumed to be entirely funded from equity. This is probably a realistic assumption for a Yukon smelter developed by one of the large aluminum producing companies.

Secondary analyses are also carried out for debt/equity ratios of 50/50 and 70/30. Debt financing would be appropriate where loans were guaranteed by government as an incentive for introduction of new industries to the Yukon.

It is assumed that equity capital would have to yield a 15 percent after tax DCF rate of return during plant construction and over the operating life. This rate of return on equity is reasonable for normal business risk.

Sensitivity analysis is also carried out for a 20 percent rate of return on equity, to reflect the possible effects of higher risks that might be associated with development of a Yukon smelter.

Annual interest on both short and long term debt is estimated at 10 percent. Debt is retired in equal annual payments over 20 years.

Note that interest rates and return on equity are tied to an assumed annual inflation rate of 5 percent (see A.6). The analysis presented would also be valid for any consistent set of conditions where interest rates equal inflation plus 10 percent (for the base case).

A.4 Income Tax

A tax rate of 43 percent is used for calculating the CRF. This rate is entirely comprised of the federal tax for manufacturing and processing industries.

In all cases it is assumed that tax deductions accruing from capital cost allowances and interest payments will be used as they occur. Generally this implies development by established corporations with a sizeable tax liability on their present operations.

A.5   Capital Cost Allowances

For the baseline case it is assumed that capital cost allowances will average 20 percent of the eligible capital investment, computed on a declining balance commencing the first year of operation. Sensitivity analyses are also carried out for calculating capital cost allowances based on a 10 percent declining balance.

In all cases 90 percent of the total capital investment is assumed to be eligible for capital cost allowances. The remainder of the capital cost, including any unclaimed depreciation, is recovered in the final year of operation.

A.6   Inflation

Financial analyses are carried out in current dollars and the results are then adjusted to yield capital recovery factors in constant dollars. An inflation rate of 5 percent is used in the calculations for all costs and revenues.

A.7   Production Revenues

The analysis is based on production revenues remaining constant in real terms (i.e. increasing at the general inflation rate of 5 percent annually). The operating lives of all plants are taken to be 20 years. It is expected that it will take about two years to reach full production; in the analysis, it is assumed in all cases that the plants will average 40 percent of full production in the first year, 80 percent in the second year and 90 percent in the third through twentieth years. The capital recovery factors are calculated to take account of this development schedule.

A.8   Capital Recovery Factors

Table A-1 shows the capital recovery factors for a range of conditions concerning debt/equity, capital cost allowance and return on equity.

A.9   Estimation of Maximum Electricity Rates

Using the capital recovery factors identified in Table A-1, it is possible to calculate the maximum electricity rates under which an aluminum smelter could operate. The results of these calculations are shown in Tables A-2 to A-9. An interpretation of the results of this analysis is contained in Section 7.0 of Chapter III.

TABLE A-1

CAPITAL RECOVERY FACTORS

Case Number	Equity	Capital Cost Allowance	Tax Rate	Return Equity*	Factor
1	100%	20% D.B.	43%	15%	.197
2	100%	20% D.B.	43%	20%	.300
3	100%	10% D.B.	43%	15%	.210
4	100%	10% D.B.	43%	20%	.318
5	50%	20% D.B.	43%	15%	.147
6	50%	20% D.B.	43%	20%	.206
7	30%	20% D.B.	43%	15%	.127
8	30%	20% D.B.	43%	20%	.168

* After tax.

Adapted from: Canadian Resourcecon Ltd., 1980. Economics of Synthetic Liquid Fuels in Ontario Road Transportation, prepared for the Conservation and Renewable Group of the Ontario Ministry of Energy.

TABLE A-2 : CASE 1

CALCULATION OF MAXIMUM ELECTRICITY RATES
UNDER WHICH A YUKON SMELTER COULD OPERATE

(millions of 1980$)

Year	Revenues	Op. Cost	Cap. Cost	Elec. Cost	$/GJ	Mills/kWh
1985	302.7	156.2	103.8	42.7	5.85	21
1986	309.1	158.3	103.8	47.0	6.44	23
1987	315.2	160.6	103.8	50.8	6.96	25
1988	321.3	162.7	103.8	54.8	7.51	27
1989	327.4	164.7	103.8	58.9	8.07	29
1990	333.5	166.8	103.8	62.9	8.62	31

Assumptions:

Aluminum prices - real increase of 2 percent per year.
Operating capacity - smelter operates at 90 percent capacity.
Financing - debt/equity - 100 percent.
Capital Cost Allowance - 20 percent declining balance.
Return on Equity - 15 percent.
Capital Recovery Factor - 19.7 percent per year.

TABLE A-3 : CASE 2

CALCULATION OF MAXIMUM ELECTRICITY RATES
UNDER WHICH A YUKON SMELTER COULD OPERATE

(millions of 1980$)

Year	Revenues	Op. Cost	Cap. Cost	Elec. Cost	$/GJ	Mills/kWh
1985	302.7	156.2	158.1	-11.6	1.59	-6
1986	309.1	158.3	158.1	-7.3	-1.00	-4
1987	315.2	160.6	158.1	-3.5	-0.48	-2
1988	321.3	162.7	158.1	0.5	0.07	0
1989	327.4	164.7	158.1	4.6	0.63	2
1990	333.5	166.8	158.1	8.6	1.18	4

Assumptions:

Aluminum prices - real increase of 2 percent per year.
Operating capacity - smelter operates at 90 percent capacity.
Financing - debt/equity - 100 percent.
Capital Cost Allowance - 20 percent declining balance.
Return on Equity - 20 percent.
Capital Recovery Factor - 30 percent per year.

TABLE A-4 : CASE 3

CALCULATION OF MAXIMUM ELECTRICITY RATES
UNDER WHICH A YUKON SMELTER COULD OPERATE

(millions of 1980$)

Year	Revenues	Op. Cost	Cap. Cost	Elec. Cost	$/GJ	Mills/kWh
1985	302.7	156.2	110.7	35.8	4.90	17
1986	309.1	158.3	110.7	40.1	5.49	19
1987	315.2	160.6	110.7	43.9	6.01	21
1988	321.3	162.7	110.7	47.9	6.56	23
1989	327.4	164.7	110.7	52.0	7.12	25
1990	333.5	166.8	110.7	56.0	7.67	27

Assumptions:

Aluminum prices - real increase of 2 percent per year.
Operating capacity - smelter operates at 90 percent capacity.
Financing - debt/equity - 100 percent.
Capital Cost Allowance - 10 percent declining balance.
Return on Equity - 15 percent.
Capital Recovery Factor - 21 percent per year.

TABLE A-5 : CASE 4

CALCULATION OF MAXIMUM ELECTRICITY RATES
UNDER WHICH A YUKON SMELTER COULD OPERATE

(millions of 1980$)

Year	Revenues	Op. Cost	Cap. Cost	Elec. Cost	$/GJ	Mills/kWh
1985	302.7	156.2	167.6	-21.1	-2.89	-11
1986	309.1	158.1	167.6	-16.8	-2.30	-9
1987	315.2	160.6	167.6	-13.0	-1.78	-7
1988	321.3	162.7	167.6	-9.0	-1.23	-5
1989	327.4	164.7	167.6	-4.9	-0.67	-3
1990	333.5	166.8	167.6	-0.9	-0.12	-1

Assumptions:

Aluminum prices - real increase of 2 percent per year.
Operating capacity - smelter operates at 90 percent capacity.
Financing - debt/equity - 100 percent.
Capital Cost Allowance - 10 percent declining balance.
Return on Equity - 20 percent.
Capital Recovery Factor - 31.8 percent per year.

TABLE A-6 : CASE 5

CALCULATION OF MAXIMUM ELECTRICITY RATES
UNDER WHICH A YUKON SMELTER COULD OPERATE

(millions of 1980$)

Year	Revenues	Op. Cost	Cap. Cost	Elec. Cost	$/GJ	Mills/kWh
1985	302.7	156.2	77.5	69.0	9.45	34
1986	309.1	158.1	77.5	73.3	10.04	36
1987	315.2	160.6	77.5	77.1	10.56	38
1988	321.3	162.7	77.5	81.1	11.11	39
1989	327.4	164.7	77.5	85.2	11.67	42
1990	333.5	166.8	77.5	89.2	12.22	43

Assumptions:

Aluminum prices - real increase of 2 percent per year.
Operating capacity - smelter operates at 90 percent capacity.
Financing - debt/equity - 50/50 percent.
Capital Cost Allowance - 20 percent declining balance.
Return on Equity - 15 percent.
Capital Recovery Factor - 14.7 percent per year.

TABLE A-7 : CASE 6

CALCULATION OF MAXIMUM ELECTRICITY RATES
UNDER WHICH A YUKON SMELTER COULD OPERATE

(millions of 1980$)

Year	Revenues	Op. Cost	Cap. Cost	Elec. Cost	$/GJ	Mills/kWh
1985	302.7	156.2	108.6	37.9	5.19	18
1986	309.1	158.1	108.6	42.2	5.78	20
1987	315.2	160.6	108.6	46.0	6.30	22
1988	321.3	162.7	108.6	50.0	6.85	24
1989	327.4	164.7	108.6	54.1	7.41	26
1990	333.5	166.8	108.6	58.1	7.96	28

Assumptions:

Aluminum prices - real increase of 2 percent per year.
Operating capacity - smelter operates at 90 percent capacity.
Financing - debt/equity - 50/50 percent.
Capital Cost Allowance - 20 percent declining balance.
Return on Equity - 20 percent.
Capital Recovery Factor - 20.6 percent per year.

TABLE A-8 : CASE 7

CALCULATION OF MAXIMUM ELECTRICITY RATES
UNDER WHICH A YUKON SMELTER COULD OPERATE

(millions of 1980$)

Year	Revenues	Op. Cost	Cap. Cost	Elec. Cost	$/GJ	Mills/kWh
1985	302.7	156.2	66.9	79.6	10.90	39
1986	309.1	158.1	66.9	83.9	11.49	41
1987	315.2	160.6	66.9	87.7	12.01	43
1988	321.3	162.7	66.9	91.7	12.56	45
1989	327.4	164.7	66.9	95.8	13.12	47
1990	333.5	166.8	66.9	99.8	13.67	49

Assumptions:

Aluminum prices - real increase of 2 percent per year.
Operating capacity - smelter operates at 90 percent capacity.
Financing - debt/equity - 70/30 percent.
Capital Cost Allowance - 20 percent declining balance.
Return on Equity - 15 percent.
Capital Recovery Factor - 12.7 percent per year.

TABLE A-9 : CASE 8

CALCULATION OF MAXIMUM ELECTRICITY RATES
UNDER WHICH A YUKON SMELTER COULD OPERATE

(millions of 1980$)

Year	Revenues	Op. Cost	Cap. Cost	Elec. Cost	$/GJ	Mills/kWh
1985	302.7	156.2	88.5	58.0	7.95	28
1986	309.1	158.1	88.5	62.3	8.53	30
1987	315.2	160.6	88.5	66.1	9.05	32
1988	321.3	162.7	88.5	70.1	9.60	34
1989	327.4	164.7	88.5	74.2	10.16	36
1990	333.5	166.8	88.5	78.2	10.71	38

Assumptions:

Aluminum prices - real increase of 2 percent per year.
Operating capacity - smelter operates at 90 percent capacity.
Financing - debt/equity - 70/30 percent.
Capital Cost Allowance - 20 percent declining balance.
Return on Equity - 20 percent.
Capital Recovery Factor - 16.8 percent per year.

APPENDIX B

RELATIONSHIP BETWEEN SMELTER SIZE AND THE MAXIMUM
ELECTRICITY RATES UNDER WHICH A SMELTER COULD OPERATE

APPENDIX B

RELATIONSHIP BETWEEN SMELTER SIZE AND THE MAXIMUM ELECTRICITY RATES UNDER WHICH A SMELTER COULD OPERATE

In Chapter III a hypothetical aluminum smelter of 170,000 tonnes of capacity was considered for the Yukon. Such a smelter would require 2270 GWh per year of electricity and would necessitate a hydroelectric plant of 320 MW capacity. While this size of smelter adequately served the purposes of the analysis, there was some concern that such a smelter might have power requirements in excess of what potential power developments in the Yukon might be able to produce. Thus, the question is asked, what is the impact of different sizes of smelters on the maximum power costs under which the smelter could continue to operate? This question is considered in this Appendix.

For purpose of comparison, three other smelter sizes were considered: 50,000, 100,000 and 150,000 tonnes per year. Calculation of revenue, capital and operating costs is based on information in Chapter III. Due to the way in which they were calculated, revenues and operating costs for the three alternate plant sizes are estimated by scaling down the revenues and costs for the 170,000 tonne smelter. Capital costs are not quite so easy to calculate as bigger plants enjoy economies of scale, especially as investments on transportation and some other equipment remain substantially the same regardless of smelter size. To account for this an assumption used in other feasibility studies and cost estimates has been employed. This assumption states that as a project is scaled up or down, the capital cost increases or decreases in proportion to the plant capacity raised to the 0.8 power. Thus, to increase plant capacity by 10 percent would only increase capital costs by about 8 percent.

On the basis of the methodology outline above the maximum power costs for the three different smelter sizes are summarized in Table B-1. The information shown is for 1985 and assumes an operating capacity of 90 percent. The real price of aluminum is assumed to increase by two percent per year. Assumptions behind the capital recovery factor used include:

- 100 percent financed from equity,

- capital cost allowance calculation uses a 20 percent declining balance, and,

- return on equity of 15 percent.

The impact of decreasing smelter sizes is that electricity must be progressively less expensive if the smelter is to remain viable. For example, a smelter of 100,000 tonnes is 40 percent smaller than the 170,000 smelter proposed but would require 25 percent lower electric power costs to be viable. Further decreases in smelter size would require even lower power costs. This relationship between smelter size and power costs is shown in Figure B-1.

With the information in Figure B-1, it is then possible to assess what size smelter would be required once the size of the potential Yukon hydroelectric projects is known. In general, though, hydro plants smaller than 320 MW would require that smaller smelters be built; these smelters must have cheaper power in order to be viable. Unfortunately, the cost of electrical generation increases as plant size decreases so that power costs for plants smaller than 320 MW will be higher. Thus, hydroelectric generating plants smaller than a 320 MW plant (necessary for the 170,000 tonne smelter) may preclude development of a Yukon aluminum smelter because electric costs are just too high.

117

TABLE B-1

RELATIONSHIP BETWEEN DIFFERENT
SMELTER SIZES AND MAXIMUM ELECTRICITY RATES
UNDER WHICH A SMELTER COULD OPERATE, 1985

(millions of 1980$)

	50,000 Tonnes	100,000 Tonnes	150,000 Tonnes	170,000 Tonnes
Revenues	89.0	178.0	267.1	302.7
Capital Cost				
- total	198.1	344.1	476.6	527
- annualized	39.0	67.8	93.9	103.8
Operating Costs	45.8	91.6	137.5	156.2
Electricity Costs	4.2	18.6	35.7	42.7
Power Requirements (GJ)	2.2	4.3	6.5	7.3
Estimated Electricity Rates				
- $/GJ	1.91	4.33	5.49	5.85
- mills/kWh	7	16	20	21

FIGURE B-1

**RELATIONSHIP BETWEEN SMELTER SIZE AND THE MAXIMUM
ELECTRICITY RATES UNDER WHICH A SMELTER COULD OPERATE**

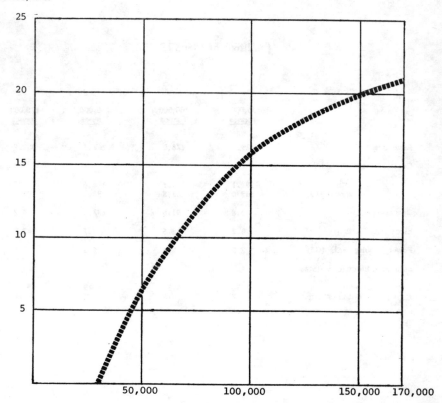

Smelter Capacity (Tonnes)